DIRECT MARKETING IN ACTION

DIRECT MARKETING IN ACTION

Cutting-Edge Strategies for Finding and Keeping the Best Customers

**Edited by
Andrew R. Thomas, Dale M. Lewison,
William J. Hauser, and Linda M. Foley**

Westport, Connecticut
London

Library of Congress Cataloging-in-Publication Data

Direct marketing in action : cutting-edge strategies for finding and
keeping the best customers / edited by Andrew R. Thomas.
   p. cm.
  Includes bibliographical references and index.
  ISBN 0-275-99223-3 (alk. paper)
  1. Direct marketing. 2. Target marketing. 3. Marketing—Management. 4.
Consumer behavior. I. Thomas, Andrew R.
  HF5415.126.D57 2007
  658.8′72—dc22   2006026009

British Library Cataloguing in Publication Data is available.

Library of Congress Catalog Card Number: 2006026009
ISBN-10: 0-275-99223-3
ISBN-13: 978-0-275-99223-1

First published in 2007

Praeger Publishers, 88 Post Road West, Westport, CT 06881
An imprint of Greenwood Publishing Group, Inc.
www.praeger.com

Printed in the United States of America

The paper used in this book complies with the
Permanent Paper Standard issued by the National
Information Standards Organization (Z39.48–1984).

10 9 8 7 6 5 4 3 2 1

Copyright Acknowledgments

The editor and publisher gratefully acknowledge permission for use of the
following material:

Excerpts from the *Direct Magazine* article in chapter 14. Direct. Reprinted
with the permission of Prism Business Media, Inc. Copyright © 2005. All
rights reserved.

For Gary and Karen Taylor

CONTENTS

ILLUSTRATIONS

Figures

Tables

Chapter 1

WHAT IS DIRECT MARKETING?

Andrew R. Thomas and Karen Nelsen

> In the business world, the rearview mirror is always clearer than
> the windshield.
> —Warren Buffett

The children don't have all that much "junk mail" to cut up for con-
fetti any longer. Their mother holds a white flag. The man opens his
e-mail without automatically moving his hand to the delete spam but-
ton. He, too, grasps a white flag. The family actually watches advertisements on television at times other than the Super Bowl. They all
hold white flags and wave them high. When the telephone rings, the
businessman knows it will likely be a call he wants to take. The fellow
in the marketing office feels good about the work he is doing. Someone proclaims, "The war is over." And someone else says, "There IS a
better way."

Simply stated, most people and organizations don't want to hear
from a marketing department. The seemingly one consistent message
yelled in the business world is that most marketing efforts have nothing
to do with the customer. It's all worse than noise. It's an interruption. It's
hostile. That's the unspoken but well-known reality for much of marketing today. Marketing broadcasts messages to people who don't want
to listen. Every advertisement, press release, publicity stunt, and give-
away engineered by a marketing department is colored by the fact that
it's going to a public that did not ask to hear it; doesn't want to hear it;
and, if given the choice, would more likely than not tune it out at every
chance.

It really seems that the marketers are out to get us. To fend them
off, we spend more and more of our time trying to get away from
them. With the remote control serving as our first line of defense, we

automatically surf through the channels the second the commercials appear. We open our mail over the waste basket, struggling to discern the junk mail without having to open the envelope. We scan through our bulk folder to see if any "real" messages were misplaced there and diligently search through our inbox to find and delete any spam that might have slipped through the cracks. We subconsciously fight the attachment of marketing messages to everything. And, yet, it feels like we cannot win. We cannot bust out and free ourselves from the grip of the marketers.

Following are some of the mistakes leaders make when approaching their company's marketing strategy:

- They wrongly assume that simply more customers and sales mark the road to profitability. They don't realize that having the right kinds of customers and sales is the way to achieve success. In other words, size doesn't matter nearly as much as quality.
- They wrongly embrace the shotgun approach. That is, if we throw enough marketing dollars against the wall, a certain amount will stick—some how, some way—which will metaphysically transform themselves into customers, profits, and market share. But business doesn't work that way.
- They wrongly assume that almost everyone wants to hear from them. In fact, very few people actually want to tune into an advertisement about their company, receive a brochure, visit the Web site, and so on. So why focus on the many? It is a huge waster of resources. It is only the select few who want a relationship with us who we should be targeting and toward whom we should be allocating our resources.

As a reader of this book, it can be pretty well assumed that you either spend your days wielding a marketing axe or are at least thinking about doing so. As practitioners, we often design expensive marketing campaigns based on tactics that bombard people with messages to penetrate markets. How ironic, then, is it that in our private lives we defend ourselves from the marketing messages out to get us? For far too many, business-as-usual has evolved to a constant state of war with the market, with the marketing department manning the frontlines.

Consider how we have evolved: Markets once were places where producers and customers met face to face and engaged in conversations based on shared interests. Now more and more business-as-usual is engaged in a grinding war of attrition with its markets. No wonder most marketing attempts fail. However, it does not have to be that way.

Figure 1-1 The Frontlines

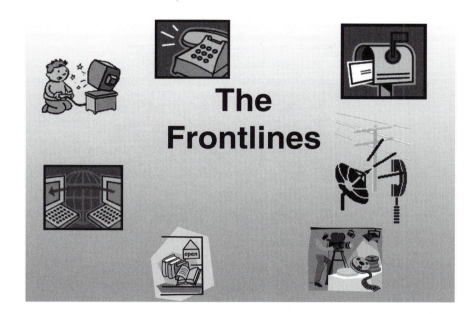

DIRECT MARKETING AS THE SOLUTION TO THE MARKETING QUAGMIRE

Marketing, like cooking, is both an art and a science. Every analyst, like every cook, has a different recipe. The quality of the result is in how well it satisfies. The ultimate objective of a marketing strategy is to provide the direction for an organization to make more money. To fulfill this objective, a sound marketing strategy must be understandable, relevant, and actionable.

Segmentation and niches seem to provide a way to do this. However, most companies have too many segments and niches to manage. And, even more disheartening, they tend to look at the wrong segments and niches. Very few marketers like to go after smaller segments and niches. Most people want to target the largest segments. There are several reasons why this strategy often fails. First, the larger segments attract the most competition. Second, smaller segments may have more distinct needs that can be satisfied profitably. Third, targeting larger segments costs more, and those costs may reduce margins more

Figure 1-2 Marketing Segments, Niches, and Micromarkets

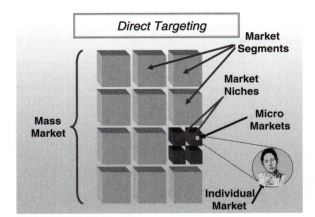

drastically than targeting smaller segments. In other words, focusing on niches and segments comes up short for many organizations.

Direct marketing, on the other hand, cuts through the confusion and uncertainty of mass marketing, segmentation, and niches and goes right to the customer. In his book, *Permission Marketing* (1999), Seth Godin provides an alternative to marketing by interruption. He calls it "Permission Marketing," which offers the consumer an opportunity to volunteer to be marketed to. By talking only to volunteers, Permission Marketing guarantees that consumers pay more attention to the marketing message. It allows marketers to tell their story calmly and succinctly, without fear of being interrupted by competitors or Interruption Marketers. It serves both consumers and marketers in a symbiotic exchange. Permission Marketing is anticipated, personal, and relevant.[1]

However, there is another level of frustration—a deeper one that people experience when encountering many marketing strategies. It is similar to a hostage situation. Hostage marketing has become the way for companies in virtually every industry to provide "customer service" to their clients. Have you ever tried to switch cell phone providers and keep your existing phone number? How about Internet service providers? We get treated more like hostages than as customers. We are locked in. We cannot leave. Moreover, we risk tremendous negative consequences if we try to escape and fail.

Again, there is hope. There are places where customers and their suppliers are getting together to communicate as real people once again. On the Internet, through Podcasts, and via text messages, markets are getting more connected and more powerfully vocal every day. These markets want to talk, just as they did for the thousands of years that passed before "market" became a verb with us as its object.

We buy books and tickets on the World Wide Web. Not over, through, or beside it. To call it a "platform" belies its hospitality. What happens via these new outlets is more than commerce, more than content, more than push and pull and clicks and traffic and e-anything.

These new outlets are real places where people can go to learn, to talk to each other, and to do business together. It is a bazaar where customers look for wares, vendors spread goods for display, and people gather around topics that interest them. It is a conversation—at last and again.

In this new place, every product you can name, from fashion to office supplies, can be discussed, argued over, researched, and bought as part of a vast conversation among the people interested in it. These conversations are most often about value: the value of products and of the businesses that sell them. Not just prices, but the market currencies of reputation, location, position, and every other quality that is subject to rising or falling opinion.

This isn't anything new, in one sense. The only advertising that has ever been truly effective is word of mouth, which is nothing more than conversation. Now word of mouth has gone global. The one-to-many scope that technology brought to mass production and then mass marketing, which producers have enjoyed for two hundred years, is now available to customers. And they're eager to make up for lost time.

In these networked markets, it is far easier to learn the truth about the products being pumped, about the promises being made, and about the people making those promises. Networked markets are not only smart markets; they're also equipped to get much smarter, much faster, than business-as-usual. Business-as-usual doesn't realize this because it continues to conceptualize markets as distant abstractions—battlefields, targets, demographics—and to view these new technologies as simply another conduit down which companies can broadcast messages.

But these forums aren't merely conduits, pipelines, or another television channel. They invite customers in to talk, to laugh with each other, and to learn from each other. Connected, customers reclaim their voice in the market, but this time with more reach and wider influence than ever. At the core, this is welcomed by customers with open arms.

SO WHAT IS DIRECT MARKETING?

Direct marketing is about focused, targeted communication with a customer to promote the purchase of a good or service. At its core, direct marketing is multichannel: It is marketing everything for everyone to everybody. Direct marketing is global: It sells from anywhere to anywhere at anytime. Direct marketing is performance based: Its measurability ensures accountability. Direct marketing builds relationships desired by customers: It is driven by the expressed needs of customers. Direct marketing is customized: It targets markets of one or more. In other words, it is the future of marketing!

Meeting standards of excellence in business has always been important, but in today's marketplace, it is absolutely essential for your company's success and survival. To meet those standards of excellence, your company and every one of its representatives in every one of its departments must have a *customer-driven* orientation and provide *customer-driven* service.

These customer-driven approaches are essential in today's marketplace. Customers will give their business to where they find the greatest value, and a company's customer-driven orientation will give them that competitive advantage.

> Direct marketing is, as always, about communicating with consumers one at a time. It's more about the consumer, whereas advertising is about the product.
> —Lester Wunderman, chairman emeritus, Wunderman, New York

MAKING SUCCESSFUL DIRECT MARKETING POSSIBLE

Many organizations find the changes in database management and communication technology to be so overwhelming that they don't know where to begin and how to compete. For those who read direct marketing as just another buzz word in an industry that is filled with jargon, it is important to know that direct marketing is not a tactic but rather a strategy. A tactic is a device for accomplishing an end, whereas a strategy is a careful plan or method. In a football game, a trick play is a tactic but a well-rehearsed plan to contain an explosive runner is a strategy. Direct marketing is a careful and well thought out plan leading to successful customer interaction. Done properly, direct marketing becomes marketing in every sense of the word, not only for large companies but for small companies as well. Consider what Michelle Toivonen of The Friendly Geeks at Genie Repros, Inc., has to say:

For The Friendly Geeks at Genie Repros, direct marketing is our bread and our butter! We are a printing and direct marketing business. We also use direct marketing to market our own company.

Over time, we've recognized that most small to mid-size business owners know they need to do more advertising. Unfortunately, many have difficulty executing the marketing plan they carry around in their head. Additionally, these clients are very price and ROI [return-on-investment] sensitive and can be overwhelmed when choosing the "best" way to advertise. We've made it our business to help small to mid-size business owners connect with their best market. The bottom line: continue selling to their current clients while acquiring more market share.

Most of our clients are grateful for the Marketing 101 they receive when they contact us for "just a postcard." We advise them on simple marketing strategies they can use immediately to more effectively reach their market and better track their response rates. We encourage them to use an integrated marketing approach by adding e-mail or a phone call to follow up their direct marketing piece. All of our advice is free to our clients because driving their sales drives our sales. We practice what we preach![2]

Marketing used to be applied to the masses. When its poor outcomes outdated it, marketing was then aimed at smaller groupings called segments or niches. Direct marketing is aimed at the individual market (micromarket). The individual market is the customer. The dentist's office calls to remind you about your appointment. The closest grocery store asks for your customer card to record your purchases. You turn 50 and receive membership information from AARP. These are all examples of the impact of direct marketing in everyday life. Very quietly, and often without much fanfare, the most visible applications of direct marketing have changed the way we go about living, and there is no evidence to suggest that the impact will lessen.

The old Yankee peddler knew his customers and in that wagon of his was almost every imaginable thing that the frontier families might need. As he traveled he listened to the people and listed their needs, so that perhaps by the next visit he might have just what they wanted to make their new dwelling a real home. Marketing has changed in that same direction—more direct, highly focused, and interactive. With improved technology today, knowing and serving the customer is both a step back and a step forward.

To create a direct marketing process, there are 12 steps. Yes, 12 steps just like Alcoholics Anonymous or Gamblers Anonymous. The irony is not lost on the creators. So why are there not 11 steps or 10? The reason is that each of the 12 steps to a successful direct marketing program is vital and cannot be overlooked.

Figure 1-3 The Direct Marketing Process

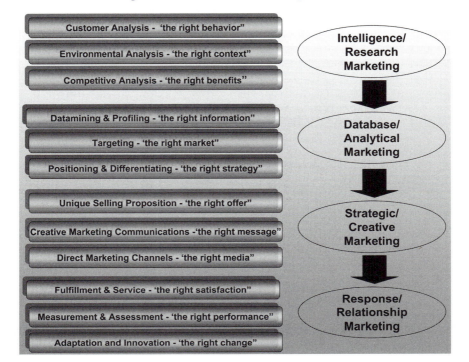

Skipping over and around steps in developing a direct marketing strategy results in something like putting on your shoes before your socks. Each step provides information that refines and directs the strategy, with the result that good direct marketing produces more results and less waste. Knowing the company, the competitor, and the product or service are key pieces of information that guide the final strategic initiative. Most important, this information enables a company to find and keep its best customers.

So what are the 12 steps?

- Customer Analysis—Profile your customer's needs, motivation, and buying profile. Ask yourself, "What do they buy, and why do they buy it?" For example, an Internet jewelry store knows that its customers don't tend to purchase expensive, authentic diamonds but at the same time would shy away from cubic zirconium. When a chance to purchase some moissanite comes along, they immediately see the value in making this offer to their consumers.

- Environmental Analysis—Companies need to proactively anticipate not only the internal needs of their business, but also the next move of their competition and competition that could potentially emerge. For example, rising gas prices shocked Americans and paved the way for a demand for hybrid vehicles that can be sold by dealers for higher-than-invoice prices. The environment provided a market for hybrids. Competitors were quick to respond with their own hybrid vehicles.

- Competitive Analysis—Find out what your competitors are doing right and what they're doing wrong. This will be valuable help in developing your own message. For example, American Environmental Products got a patent for a new light designed to ward off the effects of seasonal affective disorder (SAD) in less than half the time of current products on the market. Understanding the competition allows this company to realize why their product will be desirable.

- Data Mining and Profiling—Develop a database of prospects, then extract and analyze as much pertinent information as possible to get the best possible read on your audience. For example, customers who purchased the latest fat-busting, over-the-counter medication online received an e-mail about a newer product being touted as more effective. The computer system was designed to extract only those customers most likely to be interested.

- Targeting—Further refine your database to figure out your best prospects. For example, offer customers who are demonstrated early adopters a great deal on the latest music device, knowing that they will likely be interested and they will show off their new gadget.

- Positioning and Differentiating—Develop the offer, or central selling point, in a three-step process: (1) identify the attributes of the offer and the characteristics that make it unique from your competitor's; (2) delineate the benefits your customers will receive upon acceptance of the offer; and, finally, (3) make claims that include the promised benefits for taking advantage of the offer. For example, bankless banking is a product of the Internet. Zopa (UK) and Prosper (USA) match those who want to borrow and those who want to lend in a process that bypasses banks altogether. They charge 1 percent of the amount of the loan. The claim is that lenders earn a higher rate than a savings account and borrowers pay less interest than a credit card.

- Unique Value Proposition—Shape the statement that conveys an implicit promise of a perceived value; it will make you more desirable, healthier, wealthier, wiser, and so on. For example, FedEx tells customers, "When it absolutely, positively has to get there overnight." UPS counters with, "What can Brown do for you today?" UPS uses the word "you" to personalize the message further.

- Creative Marketing Communications—Determine how you'll shape the message you've crafted. The message package involves each component of the direct mail campaign, from the tone to the typestyle to the call to action. For example, Gatorade, one of the first

sports drinks that promised to replenish lost electrolytes, has continued to be at the forefront of this niche in the beverage market thanks
to their catchy television commercials, their colorful logo, and their
lucrative endorsements at almost every college football game. Who
hasn't seen the big Gatorade drum being overturned on the coach after a win? They have followed up with Propel and Endurance, other
drinks for sports-minded individuals.

- Direct Marketing Channels—Figure out how you'll deliver your message. By mail? Newsletter? Phone call? Choose a direct marketing
channel that will best get your pitch into the hearts and minds of your
customers. For example, David Oreck's choice is television where he
demonstrates the company's eight pound vacuum cleaner. Chadwick's,
a women's clothing company, uses a catalog along with the Internet.

- Fulfillment and Service—Let's say your prospect bites. How are you
going to fill her order or his request for a free sample or more information? Make sure your fulfillment and service operations run
smoothly and conveniently for your buyers. For example, Country
Curtains emphasizes customer service in every aspect of this catalog
and Internet company headquartered in Massachusetts. Customer
service employees are pictured in their catalog, right along with pictures of the company president. If something in your mail order
doesn't look right, they call.

- Measurement and Assessment—Track results so that you know what
you did right and wrong. Your campaign only worked if it cost-
effectively bridged the barrier between you and your prospects. For
example, Smuckers produces a line of snack products that are provided to airline passengers. They want to know whether the products
are well received and may possibly do an in-flight survey.

- Adaptation and Innovation—Revise, refine, relaunch. If you're not
totally happy with the results, don't be afraid to tinker with the message, communications channel, or any other campaign element. For
example, when Coca-Cola introduced New Coke, consumers rejected
it overwhelmingly. The company relaunched its flagship product
under a new name, Classic Coke, and advertised accordingly.

Robert A. MacKay, vice president of Internet sales and marketing for Step2 Corp., summarizes this 12-step strategy: "Direct marketing is a pivotal element of our marketing mix. It is bridging the
gap between our best consumers and the hard-to-find products they
desperately want. In the process, it is strengthening our relationships
with them and sharpening our focus."[3]

Jay Lehman would agree with that philosophy. After many trips
abroad, he saw the need to continue to produce various tools and
implements when most companies no longer made them. The family's
hardware store, Lehman's, is now the world's largest purveyor of historical products like those seen in *Pirates of the Caribbean*.[4]

Is the strategy of direct marketing right for your company? Indeed, it is. Whether large or small, all companies can benefit from this direct marketing approach. Smaller companies with fewer resources can ill afford to throw dollars to the wind, so using marketing dollars wisely is essential. Larger companies also have a bottom line for marketing costs, and in some cases, the marketing department will receive more funding when it has proven itself with a strategy that works. The 12-step direct marketing sequence is current, proactive, and understandable. In short, it's for you. Tim Searcy, CEO of the American Teleservices Association, states, "Direct marketing is the fastest growing segment of the marketing and advertising space. Without a doubt, individuals with the education and skills to master the direct marketing process as outlined in this book will have an enthusiastic reception in the marketplace."[5]

What happens when a company follows these 12 steps? The result is that the firm is bringing "good news" to their customers rather than aggravation and frustration. The result is that relationships are built. The result is that the customer doesn't feel that his or her time is wasted. The result is that you are partnering with the customer, and then he or she sings your praises to everyone who shows an interest. Direct marketing way is *the* way to bring about that kind of difference.

Chapter 2

CUSTOMER ANALYSIS: THE RIGHT BEHAVIORS

Deborah L. Owens and William J. Hauser

No matter what you sell, you've got to sell satisfaction.
—Stanley Marcus, founder of Neiman Marcus

UNDERSTANDING THE CUSTOMER: THE FOUNDATION FOR DIRECT MARKETING

Satisfying the wants and needs of customers is the underlying foundation for any direct marketing campaign. Successful direct marketing strategy, in the truest sense is designed to deliver to customers those goods and services that offer "their" preferred combination of tangible and intangible benefits that offer them the greatest overall value. If done the right way, the outcome will be a one-on-one relationship where communication messages, channels, and products are tailored by how, when, and where the customer wants them. When direct marketing is done properly, the customer will feel that you really know him or her. And, they will want to do more business and refer others to you. They will become your apostles.

The first critical step on your journey to increased market share and profits is to deeply understand your customers—how they think, feel, and act, and, how you can translate these factors into superior customer value. Sounds easy, doesn't it? But customer attitudes, needs, and actions are continually changing. Today's sophisticated customers expect that companies will meet and, at times, surpass their increased demands. Direct marketing, therefore, requires an understanding of the customer's unique needs and preferences.

A recent study by Yankelovich, Inc., found that customers want to be marketed to much better.[1] Consumers prefer the marketing to be short and to the point (43 percent); able to be viewed at the time most convenient to them (33 percent); personally communicated to them by trusted friends or experts (32 percent); and, customized to fit their specific need and interests (29 percent). Not surprisingly, most consumers (55 percent) stated they would even be willing to pay more, if they could be marketed to in ways that they prefer and control. The great news is that direct marketing offers the opportunity to meet the features that today's knowledgeable buyer wants and expects.

Through the Customer's Eyes

Unfortunately, and too often, marketing managers do not view products and services through the eyes of the customer, but through their own lens. Traditionally, new product offerings and their boilerplate direct marketing campaigns seek the bottom—by only focusing on additional features and functions that often offer little additional customer value. The good news is that the company who can effectively uncover the real (and often unspoken) needs of their prospects and customers will have a significant competitive advantage in the marketplace.

But what is looking through the customer's eyes? It means understanding that each customer perceives value in his or her own unique way. Some customers see value as price only. Others are interested only in the product's features or attributes. Yet others base their value perceptions on quality or customer service. In reality, however, most customers form their value equation around their own unique blending of price, features, quality, and service. This is where many campaigns have failed—because of a foggy or broken lens.

DETERMINING THE COMPONENTS OF CUSTOMER VALUE

There are three major components, or pillars, of customer value: (1) the cultural aspects or the parameters in which one thinks and acts; (2) the emotional or psychological aspects of the products and how they help the customer achieve a desired state; and (3) the functional aspects of the product. It is important for a direct marketer to look strategically at each of these components and see how they fit into the customer's value equation. In many cases, the customer will take some or all of these for granted and assume that you already know what they are. Many customers will say that you need to understand the culture in which they live and work. How they emotionally relate to the message or product. And then, how well the product meets their functional needs. To be successful, you must figure out the proper blending of the three.

Define the Cultural Component

Culture consists of all the material (goods, services) and nonmaterial (ideas, norms, laws) aspects that affect the attitudes and behaviors of individuals living in it. While values and long-established behaviors remain relatively unchanged, much of culture is dynamic and diverse.

It would be very misleading to view the United States as one, all-encompassing culture. The U.S. culture differs by geographic regions, ethnic groups, and diverse consumer groups. Because these factors are dynamic, the markets they influence are constantly changing. A change in one of the factors will normally cause changes in a number of other elements, all of which affect the way you do business. While it is important to understand how these elements come together to define our culture, it is essential to understand how they differ across customer and prospect groups.

Figure 2-1 Drivers of Customer Value

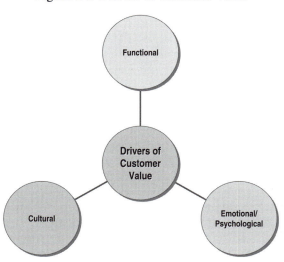

One of the first areas in which differences occur is on the geographic level. The lifestyle of a family in Cleveland is most likely quite different from that of a single person living in San Francisco. In many cases, the culture of the region will actually hinder or stop particular trends from being successful.

Next are ethnic differences. As we were growing up, it was common for us to hear that the United States was the great cultural "melting pot." That is, the best ideas, values, and attitudes from each culture are mixed into one assimilated blend that we call America. Recently, social scientists have changed this analogy from the melting to a stew pot. In the stew pot analogy, each culture adds its unique flavor to the American blend. Like a good stew, however, each cultural ingredient maintains its own identity. To someone visiting this country, we are all considered Americans; but among each other we are conscious of our ethnic backgrounds or heritage. Since the 1960s, U.S. culture has witnessed, to varying degrees, an attitudinal shift in favor of ethnic diversity. While this shift may not always be evidenced in relations among ethnic groups, it has surfaced in more subtle ways, such as trends in ethnic foods, colors, and fashion motifs.

With the increasing growth in ethnic populations also comes an increasing growth in social and economic power. Ethnic populations will continue to grow politically and, at the same time, wield more economic power. As this economic power is converted into purchasing behavior, it becomes even more imperative to understand the nuances in attitudinal, behavioral, and cultural differences in each of these groups. For example, it would be quite erroneous to view an ethnic group, such as Hispanics, as only one distinct group. Mexican culture differs from Central or South American cultures which differ from a Puerto Rican culture which is different from a Cuban one. Similarly, there is no one Asian ethnic culture (or, for that matter, European or African).

These differences dramatically influence the cultural factors that shape buying behavior. Americans of one ethnicity will look differently at products than will those of other ethnic groups. These differences are integrally linked to their cultural norms, language, and patterns of behavior. No matter how interesting or beneficial the product or service may be, if it contradicts the ethnic or cultural folkways, it will not be viewed as acceptable. The use of color in products and advertising, for example, may be uniquely defined by the ethnicity viewing it. Purple, a color that does not offend most Americans' sensibilities, is considered the color of death and only used at funerals in a number of cultures. Using this color on the wrong product or advertisement with the wrong ethnic consumer not only has negative implications for the product/advertisement, but also for the consumer's attitudes toward the company offering the product.

Language is another excellent example of the influence of regional differences on customer behavior. The history of immigration in the United States is a history of ethnic enclaves. With the settlement of these enclaves came the continuation of the native culture, attitudes, behaviors, and, especially, language. Today it is common to travel to parts of the United States where Spanish is spoken interchangeably with English. Think of your last trip to Miami or Los Angeles with Spanish as the only language in a given area.

Another key factor influencing your customer is age. Different age groups view the world differently. In today's culture, young consumers may be attracted to messages that offend older consumers. Middle-age consumers may be on the bubble between wanting to think and feel young, but, at the same time, want to demonstrate signs of respectability and maturity. Older consumers are attracted to messages that address their years of experience and their own unique needs. But, it is very important to realize that, while age is a very important indicator, it cannot be used solely to define and predict behavior. Individuals in their 50s and 60s today lead healthy and active lives. They are different than those individuals in their 70s who are beginning to slow down. Or are they?

Finally, one's position in the social and economic structure of the culture will directly influence how he or she views the message and product. Factors viewed favorably by individuals in more affluent situations may be viewed quite differently by the less affluent. For example, rising property values may please and excite an individual higher up on the socioeconomic ladder, because it will give them a higher return on their property. However, on the other hand, these rising values may hinder the individual further down the rung from moving to a better home or living arrangement.

Likewise, needs will be different across the socioeconomic groups. At the top of the ladder, there may be a need to gain even more wealth. Thus this group may follow economic trends religiously to obtain and achieve this wealth. Individuals at the middle of the socioeconomic ladder may have the wherewithal to follow some of the economic trends and not others. While they may be concerned about maintaining or growing their status, they may also be concerned about external variables (layoffs, restructuring, and so on) affecting their lifestyles and living arrangements. At the bottom of the socioeconomic ladder, individuals may be focused on surviving from day to day and are not overly concerned with many of the trends going on around them.

But it is important to keep in mind that, even within a given socioeconomic group, buying behaviors may differ depending on the individual's attitudes and needs. For example, let's look at different behavior for people buying items at a store such as Tiffany & Co., a luxury retailer of fine china and jewelry, whose customers have a need for sophisticated elegance, and superior customer service. A corporate executive may have the following demographic profile: earning more than $500,000 per year, have an MBA or law degree from an elite university, and live in the suburbs where his wife and children are actively involved in the community and youth sports. Not only will this person purchase wedding gifts for friends and family from Tiffany & Co., but also will make the purchases through a personal shopper that knows him by name, and his particular preference for sending the $175.00 lead crystal "Lydia" bowl, regardless of what the couple has registered for. This consumer is not likely to step foot in the actual store and is more likely to order over the telephone through a well-established relationship channel. After all, he does not see shopping as a behavior someone in his position would do by themselves, but within his social strata, a guest that shows up without a gift in blue box is not really in his social circle.

Now let's look at another group of Tiffany & Co. customers. This socioeconomic group consists of middle-class buyers interested in the total shopping experience. Interestingly, both of these groups share many of the same buying behaviors, which include a demand for superior customer service, being treated like "a queen/king," and having very knowledgeable sales staff, as well as on-site wrapping and repair service. The primary point for direct marketers is to realize that the middle-class shopping experience group has some very different attitudes and needs than the elite corporate executive. Members of this segment may be likely to actually visit the store, as part of a trip to the "city," or as a tourist. This group sees purchasing a gift at Tiffany & Co. as a special event. They will spend considerable time browsing in the store, taking in the pleasant surroundings of fresh flowers, and marble bathrooms, and then carefully comparing many different items before making a purchase. After having their special gift wrapped, they may decide to buy something for themselves as a memento of their Tiffany & Co. shopping experience.

Therefore, before developing your direct marketing campaign, you need to understand the different, unique cultural perspectives of your customers. Whenever possible, gather appropriate demographic and attitudinal information on your customers and use this information to create profiles that will enable you to identify and address their needs.

Define the Emotional and Psychological Component

"Wow! That product looks cool! I want it! Going to buy it!" Either the message, the product, or both have "struck your fancy," and you have become excited about possibly owning the product. You think how it might make your life better or easier, how others will think about you with the product, and that you will look and feel better owning this product. This is the emotional component of purchasing behavior. Consumers want to feel that they made the right purchase decision and that others will praise them for it. This right decision doesn't really have to be logical. It is based on "feelings" and emotions—that is, people will like me better, they'll think I am cool, or because of it, they just feel they are special.

The 70-year-old gift retailer Harry and David's is known for their high-quality fruit and nut baskets and exclusive jams and chocolates. Harry and David's understands that they are not merely selling fruit or chocolate. Chocolates are available at every mall, grocery store, and card shop, as well as at numerous other retail locations. What Harry and David's is delivering is much more significant. They are not merely selling chocolate; they are providing an experience. When a Harry and David's Ultimate Chocolate Tower arrives at someone's office or home, filled with a rich assortment of chocolate truffles and Bing cherry chocolates, it is a "rare pleasure for any chocolate lover." It says to the recipient "you are special to me, and you deserve the best that there is," or at least the best that $36.95 can buy. Therefore, the real need in this situation was "to make someone feel special." The Harry and David's Ultimate Chocolate Tower was the means to that end.[2]

A successful direct marketing strategy must identify and corral the prospects' and customers' emotions. One way of doing this is simply to ask your customers what they like and dislike and why they purchase certain of your products. So many companies seem to live in fear of asking their customers and prospects their true feelings and opinions. It really helps to find out who your customers identify with or want to be like. Who are their "reference" groups? Are they celebrities, friends, family members, or other people? What about these groups makes the customer want to be like them? Is it having the same products they use? Is it having something new and different than the people around them? Are they following some fad or trend? Make sure that you track this information and include it in your customer database so that you will have real, multidimensional profiles of your customers.

Likewise, many businesses view customer value only through the functional or operational lens without appreciating emotional dimensions of the messages and the products or services provided. For example, a supplier of polymer processing compounds to the plastics industry conducted a survey to determine the satisfaction level of current and past clients. Much to the surprise of the vice president of marketing and sales, one of the significant value drivers was the ability of the salesperson to empathize with the customer about a production problem related to compounding issues. Of course, there is a functional element: the production manager must keep the line operational and the products must flow to him. This is a given. But, in this case, the customer valued *empathy* (emotional component) much more than the *product* (functional component). What the client is saying here is that, although your product is important, what really matters is that I want your salesperson to understand me and my issues.

The production manager was not merely purchasing polymers to meet the need of certain production ingredients to produce construction joints. Instead, the manager was purchasing the knowledge, ability, and solutions of a salesperson who would empathize and help him solve his production problems if and when they arise. Products are a means to an end—not an end to themselves.

There are a number of psychological factors or drivers that can be used to help explain a customer's buying behavior. Key among these are a need to have control over one's environment, a need for affiliation or association, a need for achievement, and a need to aspire. Most individuals rely on a combination of these factors when making their decisions. By understanding the relative weight your customer places on each factor, profiles can be developed and operational tactics employed to offer unique direct marketing strategies. Whether you call it power or a sense of comfort, customers feel better making a decision when they think they have control over their environment (for example, channel, message, time to decide). For example, you can create options for your customers that allows them to decide when and how they want to receive information (mail, telephone, e-mail, Web sites, and so on) and how they want to purchase the product. Because you have gathered information on your customers' preferences, you can create customized programs to give them that control. Hilton Hotels has effectively used this approach in creating databases and profiles of the preferences of their Hilton Honors members. A silver Hilton Honors Member who likes to jog may stipulate on their profile that they want two bottles of water in their Embassy Suites Hotel refrigerator daily. Upon arrival, the guest room will have a personalized card on the desk, notifying them by name that "Based on your preferences, two bottled waters have been placed in the refrigerator for (your name)."

Likewise, affiliation or association may be a salient attribute for many customers. Many companies have effectively utilized this desire for affiliation to bring customers into the brand experience. One such option is through company-initiated electronic communities, such as blogs. IBM has effectively used blogs to help attract individuals interested in or affiliated with their Lotus Notes software. Ed Brill, the top business unit executive for Lotus Notes, operates a daily Lotus Notes blog site where users can interact and associate with other Lotus notes users to exchange ideas and comments, both positive and negative. Not only does this build on an associated community of like-minded people, but also serves as an opportunity for IBM to receive unfiltered customer feedback. Brill maintains that the 90 minutes that it takes each day to maintain this site, has more than returned that amount in new ideas to enhance the product, as well as provide positive reinforcement for users. "I have found that the one-on-one community interactions become incredibly powerful for decision making in my own job and for feedback in my own organization."[3]

The need for achievement is vital to many purchasers in both the business-to-business and consumer domains. In the realm of human resources, companies want products and services that help them achieve success, such as meeting corporate profit goals, reducing employee turnover, reducing benefit costs, or decreasing sick time. Wellcorp is an example of a company that attempts to help their clients achieve these goals. It is a fast-growing company that specializes in helping companies reduce their overall benefit costs, and improve productivity of their workforce, through the monitoring and management of staff wellness programs. Cheryl Agronovich, CEO, has found that company managers have a strong desire to achieve cost reduction goals, and thus respond well to carefully crafted messages that are customized to meet the needs of their workforce. Agronovich has credited the growth of Wellcorp to their ability to develop customized approaches to each company's unique workforce and benefit needs. Databases are then used to effectively develop client profiles to position the products and services to meet the very specific and unique needs of their diverse group of clients. For example, Wellcorp found that the exercise and nutrition programs that effectively motivated teachers in Mexico were very different than the programs that motivated Eaton Corp. employees in Ohio.[4]

The use of special offers, sweepstakes, and loyalty clubs are other ways of responding to the customer's need for achievement. An example of this would be providing offers based on product purchase patterns that reward frequent or high users of services. This may take the form of providing a mail offer, such as a free oil change to a loyal automotive repair customer, or a ticket to the professional baseball loge for a very profitable business customer. Consumers and businesses want to be recognized for their buyer behaviors in ways that demonstrate that your company perceives them to be special and engaging, and connects them with other like-minded individuals.

A word to the wise: A company must carefully understand the cultural dimensions before establishing an achievement-based marketing program. Some years back the Goodyear Tire and Rubber Co. offered a trip to Africa as a reward for tire dealers exceeding their sales targets. Unfortunately, several of those invited declined the invitation, with one telling, then–Vice President of North American Sales James Barnett, "If I wanted to smell elephant dung I would go to the zoo."[5]

Finally, customers are also driven by the need to aspire. A few years ago, Nike sold its basketball shoes using the tagline "Be Like Mike." Obviously the Mike here is Michael Jordan of the Chicago Bulls and NBA fame. What young man, or for that matter young woman, did not want to be able to play basketball like Michael Jordan and, more important, achieve his success and wealth? Effective messages provide, in the customer's mind, a means to achieve their aspirations. Whether or not the shoes make one a better player is less important than the feeling it provides. This need for aspiration is evident throughout most buying behavior. If I purchase these products (training courses), I can aspire to a better position or career. If I buy these investment products, I can aspire to a better standard of living for me and my family. If I buy this new iPod, I can aspire to be the coolest person in my group of friends. Never underestimate these needs, especially aspiration. It is part and parcel of the reason for marketing. If marketing is the engine that drives individuals to perceive they need a product or service, then aspiration is the gasoline that keeps this engine running.

Conceptualize the Functional Component

Because the customer sees the purchase as a means to an end, you must as well. Viewing customer needs as the end, and the products and services as the means to accomplish them, is an excellent tool for understanding the relationship between your business and the customers you serve. For example, Robert Pacanovsky is the founder and CEO of The Caterers by Paparazzi's, a full-service catering company located in Akron, Ohio. Pacanovsky had historically viewed his market from a product perspective in which he prepared, delivered, and served food to businesses and consumer clients for a variety of functions. These catering functions include company

picnics, executive seminars, employee awards dinners, client gather-
ings, and wedding receptions. By looking at his business from a
means-ends perspective, Pacanovsky was able profile the deeper
experiential needs of his clients. This led to not only new value-
added services but also a name change to Bravo Event Group and
a portfolio concept that more closely aligned with the emotional,
cultural, and functional needs and buying behaviors of his various
customers.[6]

One of the first things Pacanovsky did was to create a simple
means-end diagram for his catering business. He analyzed the buying behaviors of his current and prospective clients and made the
observation that most clients had significant additional functional
needs. These needs ranged from "I need help to hire someone to
sing Happy Birthday to my boss," to "I need to find a supplier of
live palm trees to create an authentic Luau Theme." After identifying
these factors, he determined that his customers' primary goal was to
"dazzle the invited guests," but neither his corporate nor consumer
clients had the time, motivation, or skills to line up the many elements of a successful event. After identifying his clients' goals, he
made a list of the key factors (means) that his company needed to
provide to help customers achieve their desired goals. Key among
these was providing superior quality food, a unique venue, visually
distinctive decorations, creative food presentations, and impeccable
service. The means-ends diagram then became a strategic roadmap
for the future. These additional functional needs led Pacanovsky to
expand beyond just a food catering business to a full-scale event
planning firm that specializes in coordinating all aspects of an event.
From hiring a Spanish-speaking wedding photographer to lining up
a swing dance instructor, Bravo Event Group has come to understand the buying behaviors of their clients.

Customers purchase products and services for any number of
functional reasons. Maybe it is just something needed to get the job
done or something to replace or update an existing line. Maybe a lot
of thought goes into the purchase decision (buying a house or
car) or very little (purchasing bottled water). Possibly, after the product or service is purchased, little or no thought will be given to it
unless there are problems. The functional component of buying
behavior is more complex than it seems. What is the customer's primary functional driver for purchasing the product? Is it cost? Is it
quality? Or is it a combination of these and other factors?

In many cases, especially, in a business environment, product
requirements and specifications will dictate what products will need
to be purchased. However, you must understand the tangible and intangible factors driving the customer to make the final purchase

decision. Given the choice between brand-name prescription drugs and their generic counterparts, why do some people choose one over the other? Do they purchase the name brands because they perceive them to be of higher quality and, therefore, are willing to pay a price premium or do they go for the generics because they perceive the quality to be the same, but the price much lower?

THE INTERDEPENDENCE IMPERATIVE

The cultural, emotional/psychological, and functional components are all interdependent in making purchase decisions. For given purchases, one component may have more weight than the others, but they are all usually there in some shape or form. The functional component may provide you with the product basics, while the emotional may affect your psychological attachment to it. All of this takes place within the cultural component that shapes how you think and act.

During the last decade, a new trend has been sweeping the funeral business industry. With the high price of funeral packages, a number of companies created what they call (for better or worse) "discount funeral packages." Functionally, these products, like other products, are discounted based on high volume participation in the program. By law, all products and services are regulated by the Federal Trade Commission and must be of the same high-quality standards no matter where they are purchased. The problem these companies faced was psychological. The word discount connoted cheap or of lower quality to many people. Do you want to bury your loved one in something cheap? In the U.S. culture, funerals are a major ritual and event in every family's life and traditionally there have been expectations of a "proper send-off." What will your friends and neighbors think of you if you use a discount funeral home?

Surprisingly, the discount trend has caught on, in fact, because of the functional, emotional/psychological, and cultural components. As the economy went into a major downtown toward the beginning of the twenty-first century, financially strapped families found that the word discount really applied to price only and began comparing costs as they would with other less-sensitive products and services. Once they found out that the quality was just as good, others were doing it, and there was no stigma attached, their emotions changed. This led to the overall cultural attitudes toward funerals changing and now buying "discount" funeral services has become socially acceptable.

SUMMARY

Understanding what makes a customer "tick" is an essential dimension of direct marketing. Building and maintaining a relationship with your best customers require that you know their needs, preferences, attitudes, and behaviors. Satisfying the wants and needs of consumers is the underlying foundation for an effective direct marketing campaign. Customer needs are often unspoken, but when uncovered can provide you with significant competitive advantage in the marketplace. Remember, customers are not buying products, they are buying experiences. They want to be marketed to in ways that are customized to their unique needs and buying behaviors. The purchases should be viewed not only as the end of one piece of the relationship, but also the means for the next step.

Fortunately, direct marketing is probably the most effective channel for providing customers the personalized marketing that they prefer. Keeping track of this information about your customers is perhaps the most critical step in the direct marketing process. To do so, build customer profiles based on differing cultural, emotional/ psychological, and functional drivers of your clients needs. Make sure these profiles are maintained and updated on a regular basis. Most important, use them to solidify your relationship with your customer. If your customers think that you are going out of your way to understand them and their needs, they will become comfortable with you and trust what you are doing, and be more willing to help you help them make their lives better. You do not want to just meet your customers' needs, nor just satisfy them. You want to exceed their expectations and delight them. In doing so, not only will you build a lasting, loyal relationship, you also will be able to use these customers as direct marketers of your products and services as they tell others about you.

Chapter 3

ENVIRONMENTAL ANALYSIS: IDENTIFYING INTERNAL CAPABILITIES AND EXTERNAL OPPORTUNITIES

Dan Rose

To thine own self, be true.

—William Shakespeare

With some liberty taken, we can apply Shakespeare's famous line to a foundational principal of direct marketing strategy: Know your company and be true to what your company excels in. Simple. Yet many firms do not truly understand their product offering, how it relates to their customer base, and how they can apply the company's core competencies to establish a direct link to these customers. Armed with this simple foundational knowledge, a company is poised to identify true external opportunities that it can fulfill. Ignoring these issues is, ultimately, a recipe for failure. Ideally, the opportunity is a narrowed niche offering that, in turn, becomes the fulcrum for effectively applying direct marketing principles.

Before we examine customer data, before we target a market, before we identify the unique selling proposition or develop our creative message, and before we determine the fulfillment services or ROI conversion measures, or other means of measuring effectiveness—before all else, we simply must understand what our company truly does best. Or rather more precisely, what the customer, prospective customer, and market believes our company excels in and how this matches up with our firm's core competencies.

Until a company objectively understands its strengths and its weaknesses, and until it understands what it truly excels in and how that relates to the market environment, it cannot be ensured of developing and implementing a direct marketing strategy that will ultimately support the ongoing growth of a profitable business.

Direct marketing succeeds because its fundamental premise is to provide the right offer, to the right audience, at the right time. It's highly relevant information to a highly targeted market. However, if you cannot fulfill your promises or fall short of the expectations you have created, the offers quickly ring hollow and no matter how much demand has been generated, in the end, failure to deliver can easily jeopardize your firm's very existence. Therefore, it is imperative for a growth-oriented business to recognize its core strengths and to build their direct marketing activities around those strengths. Let us not forget how just a few short years ago the Christmas buying season was marked by retailers touting the ease of shopping online only to find they were not equipped to deal with the logistical issues associated with direct firm-customer interaction.

THE BUSINESS ENVIRONMENT AND DIRECT MARKETING

By business environment, we mean two things: (1) the internal firm resources, and (2) external market issues a company deals with in operating their business.

Many businesses make a mistake by *reacting* to the external environment first which then creates an internal environment of constant adaptation, radical shifts in business direction, and often the loss of "first-mover" advantage (and its resulting gains in market share). Let's explore the more proactive strategy of looking inwardly first to identify those things a company does well, whether through the effective application of tangible and intangible resources (also known as "core competencies"), and suggest a better approach of being *proactive* by taking a leadership role in the marketplace through the use of your unique strengths.

INTERNAL FIRM RESOURCES

Internal firm resources include the assets, both tangible and intangible, a company leverages to develop its products or service for its customer base. Examples of both categories of these resources might include the following:

- Tangible: Physical assets, including equipment, manufacturing facilities, patents and copyrights, distribution structure, technology, and so on
- Intangible: Brand equity, reputation within the marketplace, intellectual capital and expertise, specialized skill sets, unique relationships, and so on

Outward-looking companies adopt the attitude that they are forced to continually change their business focus to "keep up" with the external environment. This can be an exhausting, profit-diminishing, brand-confusing, continual loop process for any business. Perhaps more crucially, it puts these firms behind their competition and tends to put them out of touch with their customers.

In his best-selling book, *Good to Great* (2001), author and consultant Jim Collins references an essay by Isaiah Berlin titled "The Hedgehog and the Fox," which provides an excellent illustration of the importance of not allowing the external business environment to first drive the decision-making process. "The fox," says Berlin, "knows many things, but the Hedgehog knows one big thing."[1] Putting this into a corporate context, Berlin divides companies into two groups:

> Foxes and Hedgehogs. Foxes pursue many ends at the same time and see the world in all its complexity. They are scattered and diffused, moving on many levels. Hedgehogs, on the other hand, simplify a complex world into a single organizing idea, a basic principle or concept that unifies and guides everything.[2]

The concept is simple: Truly successful firms do not set out to develop the best plan, strategy, or set of goals. Rather, they start with an understanding of what they can be the best at and build their plans and strategies accordingly.

Foxes, primarily externally driven companies, constantly move in and out of different strategies and approaches based on continually changing market pressures. On the surface, they may appear slick, flexible, highly adaptable, and able to do many things well. But below the water line, they are constantly tweaking and churning their business model in the hope of acquiring an advantage based not on their core competencies but on the latest business trend. They are constantly on the run and in constant pursuit of their next "big kill." In doing so, they burn through internal resources at a faster pace and realize tremendous resource inefficiencies. They are not clearly positioned in the mind of the market and ultimately may blend in as a "me too" with others in the business environment.

Hedgehogs, primarily internally driven companies, focus on the finite set of competencies they do best with an attitude of clarity and excellence. They do not constantly change their business model or offering. Rather, they refine it and improve it, resulting in greater profitability and output. By adopting such an approach they are better able to manage their internal resources and create greater efficiency in terms of firm performance and market share. These operations are more clearly positioned in the minds of their market. More important, they are built for long-run success.

In short, great companies identify their core competencies through contact with their customers and both sides agree with, and work toward, what the firm really does well. They know what they are proficient at and they lead, proactively and with focus, in providing their customer base with whatever matches the customer's needs and the firm's expertise.

Unfortunately, most companies, in an attempt to maximize revenue, try to be too many things for too wide a customer base. These companies seem to constantly adjust themselves to the whims and latest trends of the market. They never find the singular focus, or niche, of what they truly do best and then lead with that particular offering. Instead, they constantly adapt themselves in the hope of "keeping up" with the pack and the latest trend.

Adopt a "Quality" Perspective

According to Ira Davidson, director of the Small Business Development Center at Pace University in New York City, niche businesses are growing at a rate of 20 to 25 percent each year. "Niche startups are good in that they offer you a chance to focus all your branding and marketing in one area and expand on those core customers as you grow your company," says Davidson. "After all, when you try to be everything to everybody, you wind up being nothing to anybody—and that's the problem with ventures that are too broad."[3] In addition, the advantage of starting a niche business, provided you have an understanding of what you do best, is the increased efficiencies in identifying your potential customer base given that the firm has a clear understanding of its target market. This importance of matching your core competencies with your customer's specific needs is clearly evident: Niche ventures have a 25 percent better chance of surviving over 10 years than more general types of companies.

Direct marketing strategy encapsulates the process of finding and serving small, but high-quality, high-profit customers and designing custom-made products or services for them based on the firm's unique strengths.

An example of a company that went from trying to be all things to all people to effectively focusing on a particular niche is Andre Anthony's small custom electronics assembly company, Cougar Electronics, based in the United Kingdom. Several years ago, Andre began offering general Electronics Subcontract Assembly services to virtually any firm involved in the manufacturing of electronic products. Two years after opening his doors, Anthony's three-person company was teetering on the brink of bankruptcy. In a market in which there was clearly a demand for the service Cougar Electronics provided, the question was this: why was the firm failing? The answer lies in focusing the business strategy around the environment rather than considering where the firm fit into the market based on its unique capabilities.

Electronics subcontract assembly is a huge, highly competitive marketplace with lots of heavy hitters. With little direct experience in this market, Andre thought that his small company could carve out a big enough slice from such a huge market to make a very comfortable living. According to Anthony,

> We did get work, but only the jobs the big boys didn't want. The work was labor intensive and even with our tiny overhead we couldn't make enough profit to sustain the business adequately. We could never get the big, lucrative contracts because we weren't considered big enough to handle them.[4]

Anthony's mistake was trying to meet any type of demand regardless of core expertise, experience, or ability. The firm needed the revenue to stay afloat. Then, by chance, a niche business opportunity presented itself. A business acquaintance came to see Anthony with a sample cable and asked whether his company could produce five identical cables. The cable was for a computer. At the time, Anthony acknowledged he knew nothing about making cables and even less about personal computers (PCs), but he had the sample to work with and needed the revenue from the job. When the customer picked up the finished order, he mentioned that there were a few other dealers in the PC market who probably would be interested in having similar supplies of this type of cable—and he even provided a mailing list.

With hope to fulfill new orders, Anthony mailed out a personally written direct mail piece to the 100 plus dealers on the list. Forty-eight hours later the company had their first order for 10 cables and within seven days they had 11 more orders for 10 cables each.

Eventually, that one small mailing brought back a 12 percent initial response for orders—and it just kept building from there with week after week of repeat orders. Soon after, Anthony realized that he should focus the company's efforts entirely on this niche segment, and he dumped the subcontract work. Within weeks, they attracted another 26 new customers, and within six months, they were supplying most of the major dealers and distributors in the then burgeoning PC market.

Inside a year of focusing on one area, Anthony was selling thousands of computer cables of all descriptions, including highly lucrative custom formats, and they were being asked to provide advice on how to design cables for specific applications—they had arrived. And they were now the acknowledged experts—customer loyalty rocketed as did sales with gross profits of 50 percent or more.

Cougar Electronics was fortunate enough to back into a business niche, a strategy generally not recommended. However, they are a good example of narrowing a business focus, targeting a market, and significantly improving the profitability of the company. Cougar Electronics would have clearly benefited from understanding themselves early on relative to their business environment and realizing the potential for a market niche instead of burning through financial resources to the point of near bankruptcy.

Why is such a focused approach more often a better strategy for most companies? For one, this approach better enables you to position yourself more clearly in the minds of a fragmented customer base. This makes it is easier for your prospects to understand exactly what you offer and why they might need your services. In addition, your company is more able to be viewed as an authority within the market you are filling, and you stand a greater chance of building superior customer relationships. Perhaps the best reason to follow this approach is that it can allow companies to reduce external environmental threats and create improved efficiency from internal resources, thus lowering the cost of bringing the product or service to market. Creating such a strategy requires a company not only to excel in a particular area, but also to be able to identify those strengths.

EXTERNAL MARKET ISSUES

When we talk about a business environment, we're really focusing on two areas. First is the internal business environment, which includes all the resources and capabilities within a company that contribute to the ongoing functionality and profitability of the company. The second is the external business environment, which includes all the obstacles and factors outside the company that might impact its ability to function optimally and maximize profit.

Historically, these two areas might also be defined as controllable (internal environmental issues) and uncontrollable (external environmental issues). However, by adopting a market-driven approach to the business environment and narrowing the business focus of a company, creating accurate external forecasting tools, and utilizing effective direct marketing applications, a company can manage, reduce, or even eliminate the impact of external environmental issues.

The SWOT Analysis has been the traditional tool by which companies identify and understand their Strengths, Weaknesses, Opportunities, and Threats. As you'll read in the next chapter, it can be used for competitive analysis of other companies in a similar space. It's also an appropriate tool for companies to use to better understand themselves and the environment around them. In turn, armed with this information, companies may identify opportunities that match their internal expertise and choose to *proactively* narrow their offering and market, begin to specialize in a particular niche, and subsequently lay the groundwork for truly effective direct marketing activities.

A standard SWOT Analysis is organized within a quadrant template. The quadrants include two internal areas—Strengths and Weaknesses—and two external areas—Opportunities and Threats. When applying the SWOT methodology to your company, keep in mind that an overarching objective suggested here is to identify a possible niche market opportunity for your company to focus on and fulfill.

In conducting your SWOT Analysis, it is absolutely essential to consider perception versus reality and management versus customer opinion. Customer perception becomes reality in the marketplace. In recent years, Mercedes-Benz has one of the worst reliability records for new cars in the United States, yet they continue to command a premium price.[5] Similarly, Korean cars are viewed by American consumers as being of exceptionally low quality—an assumption that objective statistics show is false. A SWOT Analysis is only truly effective when management recognizes the connection between perception and reality and can use the results from the analysis to match firm strengths with customer opinions. Historic and current market data are useful, but there is no substitute for up-to-date external market data through which it is possible to reconcile internal perceptions with external customer opinions and "realities."

With this in mind, a common group of questions to ask when using the SWOT tool to analyze a company include the following:

INTERNAL

Strengths:

- What are your advantages?
- What do you do better than anyone else?
- What unique relationships or resources do you have?
- What ability do you have to produce your product or service at below industry-standard costs?
- What is the company brand value?
- What is your experience level and what intellectual capital do you own?
- Do you fully leverage technology to optimize your business model?

In looking at your strengths, evaluate them relative to your marketplace. If the majority of your competitors are providing personalized online customer service, online purchasing, and free delivery, then that is not a strength or advantage. It is a minimum necessity. *Most important, do any of your company strengths lead you to believe you could best fulfill a particular niche within your particular industry?*

Weaknesses:

- What could you improve?
- What aspects of your business do you do poorly?
- What do your customers see as your weakness?
- What is the company brand value?
- What is your experience level and what intellectual capital do you own?
- Do you fully leverage technology to optimize your business model?

The perception versus reality paradigm may provide the widest gaps here. While you may believe your company provides quality installation, training, and support services, your customer base may view that aspect of your company among the areas in need of significant improvement. *Most important, could you significantly reduce, mitigate, or eliminate any of your weaknesses if you narrowed your business model and instead begin to fulfill a niche segment?*

EXTERNAL

Opportunities:

- What new technology-related opportunities can you take advantage of?
- Has a recent merger within the industry created an opportunity?

- What mergers or deeper business relationships might help your company?
- Are there legislative, political, or cultural shifts that your company can take advantage of?
- What particular niche segment of your existing industry could you fulfill?

When evaluating your company opportunities, look again at your core strengths and ask yourself whether these help you identify any new opportunities. Additionally, look at your weaknesses and ask whether these help you identify any opportunities if you eliminated those weaknesses. *Most important, if you did begin to concentrate your business on a particular niche segment, what NEW opportunities could you identify?*

Threats:
- What obstacles do you face?
- Do you have debt or cash flow problems to manage?
- Does your competition have a competitive advantage?
- Are there legislative, political, or cultural threats that your company is vulnerable to?
- Are the requirements for your company changing?
- What technology-related threats are you vulnerable to?
- Do you have resource problems that will hold you back?

By identifying the threats you face as a company, you may likely identify opportunities to reduce, mitigate, or eliminate some of those threats by narrowing the focus of your business model. *Most important, reduce, mitigate, or eliminate your threats by targeting your business model.*

SUMMARY

So, how do we identify internal capabilities and external possibilities, and match these to maximize our firm's success? Consider the following summary points:

- Never adopt the perspective that the business environment is uncontrollable and full of threats to which your company must adapt
- Strive to identify the knowledge, expertise, and unique strengths your firm possesses, which make up its core competencies
- Actively and continually seek out the opinions of your customers regarding your firm and its offerings relative to the competition

- Conduct a SWOT Analysis that considers perception versus reality and internal management opinions versus customer opinions
- Create a niche market(s) by matching your company's core competencies with customer wants and needs
- Never mistake quantity market opportunities for quality revenue streams. Always know your firm's strengths and actively use them to gain competitive advantage.

Chapter 4

COMPETITOR ANALYSIS: ASSESSING COMPETITIVE FORMATS AND ADVANTAGES

Linda M. Foley

Most of us will never recognize an opportunity until it goes to work in our competitor's business.

—P. L. Andarr, marketing strategist

War and the competitive landscape truly is a battlefield. Consider this story of two local manufacturers whose factories are just about one mile apart. Additionally, they have company stores on their respective premises where their new products are sold and showcased. One of the companies has been known to send spies to the other's store to buy a dozen or so of each product and bring them back to their factory, so that they can be taken apart and analyzed to determine how the products work. It is really quite comical when you think about business men riding back and forth, up and down the same two-lane highway, with a U-Haul in tow, buying the other's products to try to get a handle on their competition. Unfortunately, if this is your method of competitive intelligence gathering, you are already way too far behind the curve to catch up.

As chapter 3 described, jumping first into an analysis of the external environment causes a firm to either pursue unrealistic objectives or invest sustainable resources in unrealistic opportunities. However, failure to fully recognize a competitor's potential is, as we all know, possibly fatal. Even coaches for athletic events know that coaching an athlete to achieve their best potential is only half of the solution. There also must be an understanding of the potential behaviors and future actions of the competing team. Simply put, an internal analysis provides a firm with knowledge about what it *can* do, while a successful competitor analysis provides a firm with knowledge about what it *might* do. Competitive analysis also provides some level of understanding about what might happen in the future.

Competitor analysis seems quite simple on the surface: (1) figure out who your competitors are, (2) figure out what they are doing, and then (3) make sure you are doing it better than them, at a lower cost than them, or different than them. However, this premise is in reality much harder than it seems, especially in today's hypercompetitive, highly turbulent environments. Additionally, in days past, it was much easier to turn on the television or read a newspaper and see a competitor's advertisement. However, with the direct marketing revolution, it is becoming much harder to determine a competitor's communication strategies. When a competitor calls a customer on the phone or sends a thank you, it is almost impossible for a business owner to find out about these strategies except via word of mouth. Also, as product lines are expanding and crossing, primarily because of direct marketing, it is becoming increasingly harder to even recognize who your competitors are.

As a manager of a small midwestern manufacturer of plastic components remarked to me, "We were so successful when we realized that we were selling products to people instead of selling part numbers to customer numbers." Business managers absolutely must be in a direct marketing mind-set these days to succeed long term and truly have a sustainable competitive advantage. Let's look in depth at each of these three seemingly simple, yet actually complex, steps of competitive analysis, specifically in the context of direct marketing. We also will discuss how these steps are radically different for a firm engaging in direct marketing. Additionally, because the recognition of the value of direct marketing is so new, firms that can engage in the following activities before their competitor can achieve a first-mover advantage.

STEP ONE: WHO ARE YOUR COMPETITORS?

Who are your competitors? This is such a seemingly simple question. To illustrate the fact that this is not a simple question, we will start with large companies with which most people are familiar, demonstrate how hard this is even for the big guys, and then amplify this problem by taking it down to smaller scale.

Imagine you run a large cable company or phone company. Can you answer the question posed about your competitors? A quick guess may produce answers like Verizon or BellSouth. What if you asked executives at *USA Today* or the *New York Times* a year ago? This question actually was asked to both companies, and they responded by describing a long list of other business newspapers and periodicals. Failure to identify competitors has turned out to be a costly error for both *USA Today* and the *New York Times*. Yahoo! News, which many felt was never going to recover after the Internet bubble burst, has over taken both *USA Today* and the *New York Times* in terms of daily readers.

Yahoo! has been able to do this through the use of direct marketing. They have been requiring users to sign up for most services since the beginning. This provided them with deep customer knowledge. Now, Yahoo! provides direct, customized news services to each individual reader. For example, readers can choose which type of news stories (local versus national), choose whether to read the story, view pictures, and/or watch videos. Likewise, Yahoo! readers also select other content that they wish to view (weather, sports, finance, and so on). Now, the other media companies are finally taking notice to the importance of direct marketing. News Corp. CEO Rupert Murdoch recently said,

> Unless we awaken to these changes, we will, as an industry, be relegated to the status of also-rans. We need to realize that the next generation of people accessing news and information have a different set of expectations about the kind of news that they will get, including when and how they will get it, where they will get it from, and who they will get it from.[1]

In other words, because of direct marketing, anyone that can find out more about your customer and their needs and wants, and satisfy those needs better than you, can be your competitor. What is the moral of this story? Competitive myopia is fatal.

This story illustrates that, in a world of cross-breeding, competitors are getting harder to recognize. Competition can come from many sources: direct competitors, category competitors, generic competitors, and budget competitors. To fully understand these groups, businesses must gain a complete understanding of their customers and what they are using their product for. To identify the competitor, we must take a brief reminder from marketing 101. Marketing transforms needs into wants. A consumer may know they need a new pair of jeans, but it is the job of the marketer to convince that customer to buy designer jeans. Your product must be defined in terms of what need it satisfies, not the tangible attributes of the product.

General Motors has a long history of not understanding this lesson. After all, GM's biggest problem lately seems to be thinking they are in the transportation industry. Contrast this to BMW. Because 80 percent of its vehicles are customized, it utilized a massive direct mail marketing campaign for the latest release of their 5-Series vehicle. BMW understands that customers are not buying "transportation." Customers are buying the full experience. They have also recognized the fact that BMW has been able to "create" this experience better than their competitors. Because the company is selling a customizable experience, direct marketing becomes their best outlet.

We can now look at this in terms of small, local companies to gain a complete understanding of competitor analysis and to identify exactly what type of product you have and what your customer is buying.

A small lawn-mowing company in Northeast Ohio took a good look at what product their customers were buying. After earning a considerable profit in the summer months and then earning nothing for the long winter months, they realized that their customers were buying convenience and a nicely manicured lawn. They wanted their yards to look nice and they did not want to waste their time doing it. What other services and products might other companies be providing? To provide the time savings that home owners wanted, many other services could be offered: spring mulching, fall leaf removal, and winter snow removal. To provide some of these services, the lawn mowing company needed to invest in more equipment, which was not an expense that they were willing to take. However, via business-to-business direct marketing channels, the owner simply got on the phone and started calling other local business owners. He was then able to piece together different services by different companies and offer the total package to customers. Although several companies might be providing the various services, the customer only needed to make one phone call and make one payment (thus, a convenience saving). The business owner was able to expand his product line and put himself in a much better competitive position. After all, he was providing services that no other single business owner could provide.

By going beyond the tradition product definition of a lawn-mowing service and utilizing a direct marketing-based approach, he was then able to build a large network of both business partners and customers. It seems cliché, but in a world of direct marketing, owners must not only "think outside the box," but also create a new, unique box when defining their products and services to define and identify their competitors. Competition can come from anywhere! To identify this competition, the executive must not only consider competing products, but also competing substitute products, as well as products that compete for the total consumers' discretionary income. A company in any one of these categories can become a competitor.

STEP TWO: WHAT ARE YOUR COMPETITORS DOING?

And almost more important, what do you think your competitors will do in the future?

So, now that you know who your competitors are, what are they doing and what are they going to do in the future? The tried-and-true formula provided by Michael Porter in 1980 nicely models the questions that need to be asked, namely, What are your competitor's goals? What are they trying to achieve with their strategy? What are they thinking about their current situation, and what are their strengths and weaknesses? Based on all these questions, how is your competition likely to respond or what are they likely to do?

These questions seem complicated and also time consuming to answer, but in some ways the answer can be quite simple if managers are creative in their approaches. When a brand new microbrewery began in Pittsburgh, Pennsylvania, in 1986, the owner was pretty

Figure 4-1 Competitive Portfolio of Responses

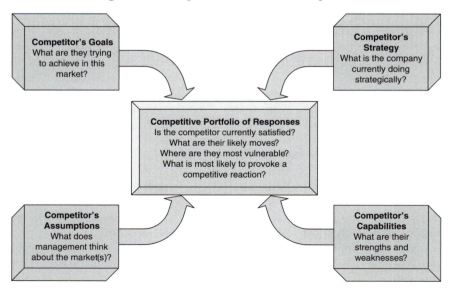

certain what strategies the main competitors like Budweiser would follow. Anheuser-Busch had been around a long time and, like many other large companies, had built a large network of distributors and had already negotiated ample shelf space in many retail outlets. Also, because the state of Pennsylvania has specific liquor laws, all beer sales must go through state stores and restaurants. So, restaurants become a more profitable outlet. Without even realizing it, Penn Pilsner took the direct marketing approach. They literally started going out and making friends with bar and restaurant owners. They provided free samples and built their new network via football tailgate parties and other social events. The strategy proved quite successful and has made the small, start-up microbrewery a booming business.

This story illustrates two things: the importance of a targeted approach and, more important, the importance of understanding your competitor. What were Anheuser-Busch's goals? What were they likely to do in the future? What were their strengths and weaknesses? Anheuser-Busch was big and over-reliant on existing channels and was basically "spoiled" and complacent when it came to securing and maintaining their existing shelf space.

To understand what competitors might do in the future, it is important to look at some of the environmental characteristics described in chapter 3. What was happening in the environment? Huge sociocultural and demographic changes were happening that made the markets ripe for microbreweries. As incomes were rising and "Generation X" reached the drinking age, consumers wanted new and different, higher-class beers. Anheuser-Busch did not send out any signals nor did they seem to be interested in developing their own line of specialty beers. As someone that served as a bar manager and bar buyer for a few years, I am well acquainted with the practices of beer distributors. As the bar buyer, I would have been happy to tell any beer distributor what the other representatives were doing and promotions that the other guys were running. Know your industry and likely industry changes by reading any and all trade publications that you can get your hands on; know your customers; know what they want in their product and from their vendors; know this by asking them and talking to them; wine and dine them if necessary; and you should be able to develop a full understanding of the competitors' anticipated portfolio of responses (CPR).

One of the most critical elements to success in terms of anticipating competitor reaction is a complete understanding of the value-chain. The value-chain includes many basic elements: (1) does the competitor have the ability to sell direct, (2) what is their extent of integration, (3) what types of relationships do they have with intermediaries, (4) what is their extent of outsourcing, and (5) in this industry and/or product line are there different channels which are available to reach consumers? A direct marketing strategy must be creative in terms of identifying and relating to all the members of their value-chain. Likewise, these are the types of things that a direct marketer must know about their competition. If a business owner can answer most of the above questions, they are probably more ready and able to anticipate a competitor's response, which leads to the next step.

STEP THREE: HOW ARE YOU DOING IN COMPARISON WITH YOUR COMPETITORS?

And, what do you plan to do about it?

The owner of a local clothing shop is not sure whether she can still compete with the "big guys." She knows who her competitors are. She knows they are not just the chain and department stores at the mall, but now also all the various options online. She also knows that with a product like clothing she is competing against everyone that sells any product that competes for consumers' discretionary income. When she does the appropriate benchmarking analysis, she always feels like she is losing. She just cannot afford to cut her margins as much as the national stores and the online stores that are selling direct. So, what should she do about it? After her recent reading of the industry's trade publications, she realizes the growing "lux" segment.

More and more people at many income levels are willing to spend more money to make themselves feel like they own luxury products. For example, the spa market has seen tremendous growth. Therefore, by combining all her sources of knowledge—(1) competitive intelligence, (2) customer and market intelligence, and (3) knowledge about her own strengths and weaknesses—she can infer that a possible solution is to ignore price competition, maybe even raise prices and target higher-end segments. The best way to do this is through direct marketing. She must use her current database of existing customers to identify their needs and increase her efforts at building and maintaining her relationships. Since the initiation of her new strategy, many customers have been willing to pay a premium to always know that when they walk in the store they will be treated like royalty, and more important, that their size will always be in stock and easy to find.

Once you have completely examined your competitors and their likely future actions, you must link that information back to your previous assessment of your strengths and weaknesses. Then it becomes a matter of benchmarking. What is your competition doing, what are you doing, and how do you compare? You now must anticipate and plan for the future. Forecasting is the key. To do this, you must develop a strategic vision for the future by asking yourself the following: What trends are occurring? How will they impact the future and future customers? How fast is the trend likely to enter and fade? Who is exploiting the trend? Who likely has the most to gain or lose? What new products will be created? Also, who are the likely future, potential competitors from companies with related industries? What future competitors are not even on today's competitive radar screen?

An owner of a small, local group of restaurants has a fairly simplistic philosophy to answer these questions. Before he opens a new restaurant, he sees where McDonald's is building a new restaurant. He told me, "I know McDonald's paid millions on the market research for that location. If they are opening a restaurant there, something must look profitable about the area. That's where I go to build my next restaurant." The theory may be a bit too simplified and based on a very faulty assumption—that is, that McDonald's knows what they are doing. However, the idea really makes a lot of sense when you think about it. Where is a lot of building happening? Are there a ton of new subdivisions being planned? Is a new interstate coming through? Those are the kind of questions that can be easily answered and say a lot about the environment. Then, ask yourself, am I there? Am I in the middle of this growth? How can I get in on it?

It cannot go without saying that you have to compare your competitive and industry analysis to what you are doing and what your goals are. Just because McDonald's is building a restaurant it does not necessarily mean that it makes sense for you to build in the same location.

I recently did some consulting work for a third-party logistics firm. They had just begun two new promotional campaigns. One was a targeted direct marketing campaign and the other involved a sponsorship with NASCAR. Their reason for beginning the sports sponsorship was because one of their major competitors had done the same. I quickly (and nicely) asked them to explain the planned objective from this campaign. The answer was something ambiguous like, "to increase sales."

However, doing it just because your competitor is doing it is not a suitable reason. If you have reason to believe that the majority of your customers are NASCAR fans, and that NASCAR and your company are good images in their eyes, then you may want to consider this possibility. Also, it is necessary to understand whether you are in the type of industry in which a mere increase in recognition could possibly increase sales. In some mature industries, the product recognition already exists and is not the problem. The problem may lie in something else like brand image or loyalty. It is crucial to know who your competitors are and what they are doing, but the third and final step is relating all that information back to your company and what you do best.

Future competitors are more likely to enter when industry is attractive. To simplify the economic model, how easy is it to get into the industry and how much profit potential is there? Going back to the McDonald's example, how much money does it cost to build a McDonald's, and is there a new mall coming in across the street? Then considering your business, how much would it cost for you to build a new restaurant in a similar location? If you do not have the financial means at your disposal that McDonald's has, the answer is that it will cost you considerably more money. But, the true answer boils down to this: The companies that are most able to recognize and adapt to these environmental and competitive future changes will likely be the most successful.

When I was working for Warner Bros. Records, I found myself in a bit of a dilemma when I needed to find some willing distributors of our "western" records. By western, I do not mean country-western, or even the old-time country music, but instead, real cowboy music. I examined what we had done in the past and what the competitors were doing, and those efforts can be summarized in two words: Tower Records. That is all we were capable of thinking about. Do the meet and greets at Tower Records, get Tower to carry it, and if it sells, it sells. By understanding my competitors past and likely future moves, I was able to surmise that any kind of risk taking would be unlikely in the near future. Because I did not have much to lose, I started calling ranches and other tourist spots where people go and pretend to be cowboys. I had a small plexi-glass display unit made that could be placed anywhere, like a front desk, and sent it out along with a bunch of promotional CDs and tapes. In six months, sales increased by 300 percent. Those are some astonishing figures when you process them—all achieved by some creative direct marketing. Direct marketing works, but you have to do your homework first.

There probably was not a huge amount of sales potential at the ranches that I targeted. However, I was the only one there and they were, quite frankly, flattered to have an executive from Warner Bros. call them on the phone. By the end of the next century, I am almost certain that everyone will have realized the direct marketing advantage. If they have not, they will probably be out of business anyway. Therefore, the one last point that needs to be made is that if you can develop a successful direct marketing program before your competitor can, you will have the competitive advantage.

SUMMARY

In the words of Sun Tzu, "If you know the enemy and know yourself, you need not fear the result of a hundred battles. If you know yourself but not the enemy, for every victory gained you will also suffer a defeat. If you know neither the enemy nor yourself, you will succumb in every battle." And also, "In peace prepare for war, in war prepare for peace. The art of war is of vital importance to the state. It is a matter of life and death, a road either to safety or to ruin. Hence under no circumstances can it be neglected."[2] You have to know your business and your competitors, and be ready to "fight" at all times. If you are reading this book, you already understand the tremendous importance of being proactive. You already know the pivotal importance of direct marketing and its benefits. A carefully planned and executed direct marketing strategy is the wave of the future. Gaining an understanding of how your competitor is or may be using direct marketing in the future is a critical component of this planning process. There are three necessary questions to ask in this process:

- Who are your competitors?
- What are they doing?
- Is your company doing it better than they are, at a lower cost, of in a different way?

After these questions are posed and answered, a marketer can then understand not only what their business can do now, but also what they might do in the future. This involves a solid understanding of your company's goals and objectives and then the ability to transform this understanding into a well-crafted direct marketing strategy, which can by itself be a first-mover advantage, and almost always will be a sustainable competitive advantage.

Chapter 5

DATA MINING AND PROFILING: THE RIGHT INFORMATION

AnneMarie Scarisbrick-Hauser

> We have only two sources of competitive advantage: the ability to learn more about our customers faster than the competition, and, the ability to turn that learning into action faster than the competition.
>
> —Jack Welch

Twenty-first-century marketing is a world of customer information, databases, and shrinking campaign delivery timelines. The old adage of "know your customer" has taken on an urgent new meaning with the exploding volume of data that are being collected, in many different databases, on each customer, every minute of the day. The need to quickly respond to market changes has increased demands on direct marketing teams to deliver "just-in-time" customer information to gain that competitive edge ("customer" applies equally to retail and commercial examples throughout the chapter). Unfortunately, there is no magical black box into which you can feed the information, and, *shazaam*, a fail-proof, individualized client plan pops out. This would be great, but the costs would be astronomical, especially for small to mid-size businesses.

Even if you have data, what do you do with it? Extracting information from a database only leaves one with a large pile of facts and figures unless it is converted into something useful. Analysis is a good first step, but it doesn't mean much unless you can make the information *actionable*. *Actionable intelligence* requires not only analysis and interpretation, but more important, integration into the context of business decision making. Only by taking the information and placing it in an appropriate business, competitive, and socioeconomic environment does one truly mine the "golden nuggets" out of the databases. Let's also not forget the value of using quality data in direct marketing campaigns, increasing our confidence that we are targeting the right customer through the best channel with the most attractive offer. An ongoing process of evaluating and improving the accuracy and completeness of the data used in analysis combined with the timing of delivery may well prove to be the missing link in gaining competitive advantage in today's fast-moving markets.

Smaller to mid-size companies do not generate, nor do they need to, the mega-size customer information databases that large corporations need. However, regardless of company size, internal customer databases may not have been designed to do anything other than record customer information, orders, transactions, and dates. Finding that "buried treasure" to generate new profitable campaign revenue becomes a challenge. Fortunately, there are many examples of tried-and-true, simple, but effective, database strategies designed to enable marketers to create customer profiles and, more important, establish actionable customer knowledge without spending enormous amounts of money.

Data analysis is a critical part of the direct marketing process. Marketers are trying to create actionable intelligence about customer behaviors, demographics, interests, motivations, potential next purchases, and, most important, the potential long-term value to our customers to enable informed directing marketing creative and campaign decisions. The faster we can centralize and maintain this customer intelligence, the better our position to deliver actionable information to the direct marketing teams to respond to timely market events, generate revenue, and increase our customer base through our customer-centric approach.

WHAT IS DATA ANALYSIS?

Data analysis is known by several different names today: analytics, statistical analysis, and data mining. Let's see whether we can differentiate what these terms mean even if they are used interchangeably today.

Analytics is the term used today to cover any type of analysis of customer data, including retail, commercial, and purchased demographic data, using a variety of statistical tools. Analytics also refers to an emerging set of skills and proficiencies expected of undergraduate and graduate business majors. These skill sets enable business majors to conduct "slice-and-dice" analyses, a deep detailed analysis of customer information used to identify niches of market opportunities with anticipated profitable return. Analytics also includes qualitative analysis of data, for example, content analysis of customer service call conversations, customer surveys in malls, analysis of frequent flyer mile usage, Web blog content, e-mail channel activity, club memberships, e-mail communications, and other channel information not captured electronically.

Data mining is an automated analytical process, processing large databases searching for global patterns of behavior, customer attributes, contact history, or campaign response analysis across millions of rows of customer behavioral data. This type of analysis has been in place in large companies for decades and is an expensive item. Customer data can be processed into segment groups or clusters of customers displaying similar characteristics. Using predefined algorithms or business rules, customer data can be processed and scored to distribute targeted offers or discounted rates to specific customers. Purchased customer "demographic" or "firmagraphic" data can be appended to customer records to provide additional historic information not readily available in company internal databases. One of the disadvantages with this type of analysis is that, because of the macroscopic level of analysis, it lacks links with the emotional measures of a customer's interaction, for example, self-reported attitudes, preferences, and measures of customer satisfaction, that may not be easily integrated into the data mining procedures. However, data mining, in its true form, does not provide the best data analysis when assessing creative ideas. It is better here to use qualitative analytic procedures.

The statistical analysis process can be used with large databases, but the procedures are most successfully used with great success on samples of the large databases by incorporating sampling methods and hypothesis testing. Statistical analysis tools—for example, Statistical Analysis System (SAS), Statistical Package for the Social Sciences (SPSS), or Microsoft Office Suite Excel pivot tables—are designed not only to work with the mega-size databases, but also to standardize and consolidate data from a variety of sources (that is, behavioral, attitudinal/emotional, as well as demographic data) into one data set suitable for analysis on desktop or laptop computers. Unlike data mining activity, statistical analysis tools are designed to test hypotheses or "test-and-learn" scenarios to discover, understand, and predict quantifiable patterns of customer and prospect behavior. Statistical tools for the personal computer are designed to be easy to learn and use. Sampling smaller groups of data permits faster analysis and testing, which leads to timely implementation of marketing campaigns.

The results of the analytics process enables direct marketers to develop marketing programs and strategies, test customized creative ideas or marketing programs, modify and implement campaigns across multiple channels, measure response results, and refine future marketing programs.

TYPES OF DATA ANALYSIS

So what kinds of information can data analytics generate? From the retail perspective, by studying their purchase behavior, data analysis can help us understand which customers may be closing their accounts or losing interest in our products. These types of studies are known as retention, attrition, or churn analyses. As you know, it costs more to bring a new customer into the business than it does to hold onto one. However, in some cases, the costs may be higher to retain a nonprofitable existing customer. Therefore, you would like to know which customers are worth the retention incentive and which are not. Likewise, it is interesting to study the characteristics of clients who have left the business. Sometimes, through analysis, you find that some client behavior costs you more than the profit you expected to make. This information enables you to make fact-based decisions related to types of customers whose business you encourage. So what else can analytics do for your direct marketing business?

Data analysis can profile or describe customer behavior over the past month or longer, depending on your needs. Looking at the commercial customer, descriptive profiles are the stepping stone to another form of analysis, clustering, in which customers are grouped together by self-similarities like sales volume generated, SIC (Standard Industry Classification) code, similarities in the seasonal pattern of orders, and so on. Commercial data also have a unique characteristic in that a business can be a company in its own right and also a parent company of many other companies. Therefore, commercial data require careful assembly of the analytical database before analysis. Customer and prospect data analysis using profiles and descriptive analysis can also be leveraged to understand how best to assess the target prospect potential as a profitable customer. Using the results of analysis, customers can be segmented into groups that will be offered different services, different fees, or different rates depending on their estimated profit value to the company. Understanding the life-cycle patterns of customer behavior, particularly commercial customers, helps you to position your marketing strategy with the right offer at the right time. Response analysis, usually conducted during and at the end of a campaign, is designed to tell you how well the marketing campaign and test campaigns performed and is a valuable measure of your successes in terms of dollars and effort.

THE VALUE OF DATA ANALYTICS

The use of data analysis is as old as the calculations used to build Egyptian burial chambers, translate the size of a Roman citizen's property into property taxes, or etch a data dictionary on the Rosetta stone to enable translation of ancient Egyptian hieroglyphics. Until a couple of decades ago, data were stored primarily as evidence of a transaction and not in a format suitable for analysis. I remember being asked to create an easier way to access student transcripts for analysis in the late 1990s and my shock when I discovered that every student's four years of academic records were spread across sixteen different backup tapes that would need to be loaded in their entirety to begin the investigation of the data. The unloading of the data from the tapes to the main computers took a week and identifying the location of the data took another few days and so on. Thanks to the advent of faster processing personal computers today, data can now be stored, imported, or exported relatively easily to SAS, SPSS databases, or Excel spreadsheets within minutes.

There are a number of tangible benefits that focused data analytics can bring to direct marketing. Let's consider three factors—intimacy, accuracy, and immediacy—and the role they play in successful direct marketing activities.

Intimacy

"Making the connection" with the customer is one of the successful keys to creating a successful customer relationship. To create and maintain this connectivity, a readily accessible timely flow of data about the customer's behavior, preferences, perceived needs, beliefs, and attitudes needs to be gathered and maintained in a centralized location. Small businesses are very familiar with this process, although many small business owners will still tell you that they keep this information in their heads and take pride in their ability to "know their customers" without electronic assistance. What about you, do you have a special store you go to for wine, or flowers or golf supplies or something else? When you visit the store, do the store owner and staff know you by name, know your special brand

and interests, and sometimes even call you at home to tell you that some of your favorite products have arrived and have been placed on hold for you? Relationship management like this surely increases the likelihood of your retention as a customer.

However, companies grow, and the need for an analytical database increases as that emotional connection with the client seems to become more difficult to sustain as a one-to-one relationship. When asked recently to explain the steps taken to recover lost business, Charles Schwab singled out the loss of emotional connection with the client that he attributed to impersonal marketing tactics of raising fees and rates, which resulted in the loss of customer referrals to new business, a situation that he feels has been remedied today by going back to the basic tenet of his business—namely, meeting the customer's needs.[1] The ability to offer quality customer service today depends on the breadth and depth of knowledge a company can store and access in a timely manner about their customers. More important, analytical data does not substitute for the emotional connection with the customer, it is one of the tools to enhance this customer intimacy.

Data analysis provides the structure and process to create and maintain an analytical database designed to enable direct marketing teams to create, strengthen, and maintain our knowledge of and connection with our customer consumer behaviors. In addition, this intimate knowledge of our customer enables us to continuously change to stay ahead of or current with customers' changing purchase intentions or relationship changes.

In 2004, Dunkin' Donuts decided to redesign their store menu panels with assistance from their customers. With the help of Design Forum, a retail design and strategy firm, Dunkin' Donuts undertook this creative activity by leveraging customer-driven data analysis. Consumer judges were asked to rate four menu board designs through consideration of a number of panel design attributes such as panel colors, fonts, pictures, pricing information, and layout. Using SPSS (an analytics data mining package) and a test-and-learn approach, customers rated four versions of menu panel designs for which each version was redesigned with customer input. The design firm used analytics to track and validate customer preferences, ratings of attributes, and comparison results. According to the design firm at Dunkin' Donuts, the information generated by the customers served two purposes: first, the redesign rating exercise identified customers' preferences, key components in the sales decision; and, second, the results of the redesign preference testing provided useful information for the validation of design proposals with company management, quantifying the risk in the proposed investment and sharpening target marketing approaches. Overall results from the customer judges indicated improved satisfaction scores with each enhanced version of the menu panels and appeared to indicate a successful outcome leveraging customers' preferences as part of the analysis.[2]

Accuracy

Confidence in the accuracy or quality of customer data we have collected or purchased is an important success factor in direct marketing campaigns. Quality means more than having the accurate name and addresses of customers, it involves adding additional information to the record when available, scanning the information for errors, locating missing data, and knowing the date of the most recent transaction with the customer. Unless all the data necessary for our understanding of the customer is located in one database, it is difficult to have confidence in the quality of that data. For example, take out your wallet or purse, count how many credit, identification, department and grocery store, medical, and other types of cards you carry in your wallet or purse. For each of these cards, a database exists containing similar, but not necessarily the same, information about you as a customer. Look at each card and see whether your name is spelled the same on each card. In my own case, hardly any of my identification cards or my credit cards display or record my actual legal name because of different data field length rules in various databases, a mechanical requirement. My own bank cannot record my legal name on my ATM card and my driving license cannot fit my first name on the card without chopping off half of my last name. I have learned to spend time reviewing my credit record at regular intervals because of the errors that have occurred.

Credit scoring companies today consolidate all the information from various databases related to the use of those cards to build a holistic picture of your use of credit, continually analyzing your behavior, related to the use of those cards, and refining a credit score that directly affects the interest rates you receive when taking out new loans. How confident are you now that each database contains accurate information when considering your credit score these days? It might be interesting to order a free copy of your report to see what it says. In the absence of any challenges from you, the customer, the credit bureaus will be confident of their results and pass this information (correct or not) on to the lenders.

Unless specific data quality efforts are included in the data preparation process, the data will be analyzed irrespective of the errors.

Maintaining quality data entails regular checking and data correction. How many direct mailings or e-mail communications do you think have been returned unanswered to your business because of mailing list errors? Do we take the time, or do we think is it too expensive, to assess and fix the data errors at their source and when we are appending the database? Do we have a continuous monitoring program assessing our data quality before we use the data as a driver of direct marketing decisions? The value of our relationship with the customer increases when we establish a culture of quality around the collection, storage, modification, and maintenance of our customer information. It is not difficult to create a quality database. However, it is far more difficult to correct data quality errors afterward.

The Six Sigma philosophy focuses on the creation of error-free business performance. Six Sigma has established a standard of 3.4 problems per million opportunities. The Six Sigma process focuses on a systematic approach to data quality and many of the steps outlined to design or create a quality process have many direct applications to direct marketing.[3] Table 5-1 briefly summarizes the similarities between Six Sigma and a typical direct marketing campaign.

Immediacy

Thinking now about how quickly data analysis can be produced and processed into actionable information, let's take a look at the next factor, immediacy. "Right time" availability of quality customer information means that the sales force is enabled to use or document the most accurate timely customer information (retail or commercial) based on an understanding of their clients' needs, preferences, and lifestyles to create an attractive customer offer. In some cases, companies seek to create the sense of immediacy associated with their products to provide a customized customer experience and also to capture as much market share away from competitors as possible. Have you noticed that the Christmas holiday marketing programs are starting earlier and earlier the past few years? Careful planning and data mining goes into testing various marketing activities, targeting programs, and timing sales by using historical data from the previous year. In addition, test results from ongoing marketing programs provide timely information to continue or change programs to achieve goals.

Think back to the last marketing campaign you put in place. Were you satisfied with the time it took to get to market with a

Table 5-1 Six Sigma for Direct Marketing

Six Sigma DMADV	Data Analytics for Direct Marketing
Define • Goals of the design activity • Identify what is being designed • Why? • Test that goals are consistent with demands and enterprise strategy	Define • Objectives driving direct marketing team • Research questions of interest • Prioritization of research questions
Measure • Determine Critical to Stakeholder metrics • Translate customer requirements into project goals	Data • Establish sources of data for analysis • Collect data into centralized dataset • Evaluate data quality and compliance with privacy
Analyze • Options available for meeting goals • Determine performance of similar best in class designs	Analysis • Analysis of data • Descriptive statistics • Hypothesis testing • Results interpretation • Deliver results to direct marketing teams
Design • New product, service, or process • Use predictive models, simulations, prototypes, pilot runs, etc. to validate the design concept's effectiveness in meeting goals	Implement and test • Direct marketing campaign launched • Test and learn activities monitored • Output/Performance data collected for analysis
Validate/Verify • Design effectiveness in the real world	Confirm • Measure Performance against expectations • Estimate Return on Investment (ROI) • Celebrate and measure successes • Confirm and address weaknesses

well-planned campaign? Were you able to save a customer relationship with an appropriate offer using fact-based timely information?
As we shall read later in the chapter, it takes time to find the relevant customer data, prepare the database for analysis, and analyze
and prepare findings to distribute to a marketing campaign team.
The faster you can get a well-planned direct marketing offer into the
marketplace, the greater the likelihood of increasing revenue and
expanding your customer base. Likewise, a well-prepared customer
information process will increase the likelihood of faster time to
market.

Losing customers is part of any business, but when attrition of
clients, or "churn," steadily increases, it can be advantageous to
understand the reasons for the smoldering signs of change before
the fire starts. Let's look at the recent changes taking place in the funeral business and how casket makers have changed their business
strategy in response to market changes.

Looking back at the funeral business, cremation rates have risen
to 30 percent of all funeral arrangements since 1970 and are set to
rise to 45 percent by 2025, leaving casket makers to reengineer their
business strategy. Companies producing caskets reviewed marketplace trend analyses and confirmed the presence of this increasing
negative impact on their business. Attitudinal research, gathered
through surveys, indicated that, as a potential new target market,
Baby Boomers are waning in their support of "traditional" burial
rituals and are more likely to embrace a small, beautiful ceremony.
Company executives considered the results of the analysis presented
and decided to recognize the growing market opportunity. They
then set about "losing" the traditional casket business to their own
new cremation business initiatives. Their timely response to market
changes will enable them to transition with less turmoil to the new
business model over the next 20 or so years.

The timing of the research provided these companies with
actionable information used to recognize the need for innovative
ways to continue to satisfy customers and stay profitable. The
industry's major players have introduced their own cremation
product lines, ranging from basic cardboard boxes to $12,000 one-
of-a-kind urns. One company, Batesville, has produced a Pottery
Barn–style cremation mail catalog with a cover depicting a purple
flower blooming from a keepsake urn.[4] Their marketplace analysis
identified two potential target markets on the west coast and
Hawaii, which has the highest cremation rate of 67 percent, followed by Washington and Nevada with 67 and 65 percent, respec-
tively, as they launch markets for their new cremation product
lines.

READY, CAMERAS, ACTION: STEPS TO DATA MINING

Step 1: Define Objectives

The starting point for any data analytics exercise is a good understanding of the overall marketing objective. You need to identify the questions you want to answer through data analysis before creating the database. Why? If you understand the context of the question, then you can focus the research activities and locate the data points to conduct the analysis. Ask yourself what are the burning questions (no more than five) that you would love to answer about your business, but that you haven't been able to resolve because you cannot access the data to do the analysis? Here are some examples of questions ranging from simple basic questions to complicated questions requiring years of analysis. Remember, however, sometimes we find that we don't have answers to the most basic questions about our customers or the performance of our marketing campaigns:

- What are the demographics of the customers reached by your latest campaign?
- Have any of your customers received more than five campaigns in the past year?
- How many customers have you lost in the past six months, two years, five years?
- How many customers have purchased more than one product from you?
- Which channel or channels do your customers use?
- What were the campaign results in dollars earned on your last campaign?
- How long have your customers owned their businesses?

Once you have identified your objectives, prioritized the list of objectives, or aligned objectives with overall company goals, you are ready to proceed with database construction and analysis.

Step 2: Establish Database, Data Collection, and Data Quality Evaluation

The one thing we are not short of today is data. One of the main problems is that the data may not be accessible in a format ready to use for analysis and decision making by direct marketing teams. In

the past 10 years, there have been major improvements in the con-
solidation of data into single locations through the development of
data warehouses designed to store large amounts of customer data
and the increasing demand, especially by legal entities, to store historic data for future review. Before the advent of the Internet, a
macroscopic-level analysis of large internal company customer databases, focusing on parsing and searching for general patterns of customer behavior related to product purchases, sustained large
company's direct marketing activities for years. Usually, the searches
produced large lists of customers' names and addresses listed by the
products currently held and potential new products to be used in
outbound telemarketing or mail campaigns. With the relative low
cost of Internet advertising, today's data mining focuses on a more
microlevel analysis, designed to provide customized information
about targeted groups or segments with identifiable needs that may
or may not fit the target market profile.

The main objective of data analytics is to organize, analyze,
interpret, and publish the most valuable intelligence about our customers or prospects that seem to share the same characteristics as
our most profitable customers. Whether looking at retail or commercial customer data, you are interested in learning more about your
clients, their needs, past purchase behaviors, demographics, attitudes, preferences, and beliefs with a view to better understanding
your target market audience.

Smaller to mid-sized companies do not need large data warehouses and can conduct their data mining activities using small serv-
ers or databases populated with a smaller collection of data to meet
their needs. Some smaller companies are setting up "data co-ops" to
load their data, paying a fee for shared access to purchased data
such as demographic customer data or informatics and business demographic data. Smaller companies can purchase Web site traffic
information from Web advertisers and create lead lists from various
opt in programs offered by Web site browsers today.[5]

Ask yourself whether you have a database available for your use
today that will allow you to sort and analyze data to answer your
research questions. If yes, then all you will need to do is verify the
sources of data necessary to conduct your analysis and add the data
to your database to meet the needs of the analysis. Remember that
you may have already collected input data or variables representing
customer behavior, attitudes, and demographics to answer these
questions, but your database may need to add some additional data
fields to create reports of business performance, known as output
data fields, variables, or performance data fields. Examples of input
data fields you might be interested in adding to your database

include the following: sales volume, SIC code, gender, occupation, number of employees, number of transactions, volume of spending on products, product suites, subscriptions, memberships, social activities, age group, social profile, and transaction dates. Examples of output data fields include purchase date, contact history information, application date, and other data indicating performance measures.

If you do not have a ready-made database, the best plan is to create an inventory of what data and information you have internally and what data you use from external sources. Once you have identified the sources of data required to support direct marketing activities, you can plan the creation of your database. As you centralize the data, you will be creating a database of organized data points based specifically on your business needs. You will also plan to add new data and information as necessary to meet business needs. Additionally, your database should be designed to support a reporting tool, such as Microsoft Office Excel, SAS, or SPSS, which will allow you to not only analyze the data quickly but also produce graphic representations of the analysis ready for use in preliminary reports.

Step 3: Analyze Data, Interpret Results, and Distribute to Direct Marketing Team

Let's look at some of the key activities associated with the data analysis. First, you will create profiles of your current data, planning to create a detailed picture of each and every client (retail or commercial) with the intention of summarizing the data pertaining to your clients in a meaningful way. Second, not only are you interested in the creation of an up-to-date single record of customer data, you are also interested in establishing an accurate trail of historic information with this customer. Once you have created the necessary data for analysis, you will use descriptive analysis, applying frequencies or hypothesis testing, and use statistical analysis techniques to test the scenarios or research questions posed by the direct marketing team.

However, you may not currently have skilled personnel at your company to conduct this analysis. Consider asking your local business school for assistance through internships or consulting services to get your data analytics process up and running. Students really appreciate real-life problems to work on, and you gain by having the benefit of their analytical skills. After you have decided the breadth and depth of analytical skills you require to support your direct marketing programs, you can decide whether to create a small group in-house to do the analysis or retain a consulting organization on an as-needed basis.

Once the data analysis is complete, your direct marketing team or analytical experts will review the results, write a report, and/or create graphic representations of the data to explain the data and answer the research questions posed at the beginning of the analysis. Place the database and research results in a safe storage area for review and validation later. Distribute and present the research finding to the direct marketing teams.

Step 4: Implement a Campaign with Test-and-Learn Cells

After the direct marketing teams have reviewed the data, they will decide how to incorporate the information into their campaigns. Data analysis can again play a role in assessing the benefit of these programs through the use of "test cells" or control groups who do not receive any special treatments from the direct marketing campaign but may decide to purchase the product for other reasons. Ideally, the campaigns should include a number of test-cell campaigns designed to identify differentiation in responses by campaign participants. However, statistically valid test-and-learn activities are not easy to implement, particularly for small companies. Fortunately, small business Web sites are continuing to discuss ways and means of incorporating the best practice of test-and-learn with small sample sizes into small business direct marketing analysis so this practice should increase over the next few years.

Following the implementation of the marketing campaign, how do you know what worked or did not work? It is essential to perform additional evaluation on the results of the campaign during, after, and at regular intervals following the end of the campaign. The results are compared against the expected results estimated before the campaign started. During the campaign, this provides benchmarks that tell management how the campaign is proceeding, and, most important, this allows the marketers to make necessary changes to improve the results of the campaign. Measure your results at the end of the campaign to give you a final picture of what was and wasn't accomplished. Follow up with measurements at regularly scheduled intervals after the campaign ends to provide additional information on the longer-term affects of the campaign. Above all, celebrate the winners and analyze the losers. But do not discard this information and analysis. Instead, include it in your company's knowledge-base to reveal lessons learned for future direct marketing endeavors.

SUMMARY

Database development and analytics in the ever-evolving age of information technology is no longer just a nice-to-have tool for businesses, no matter how large or small. It is essential for success! Each customer is a source of unique information that can help you improve your business. Knowing your business and your customers provides you with a ready framework in which to gather their information. Take the time to decide the most important information you need and then make the customer feel comfortable that the information is being used to serve him or her better. It creates a win-win environment. Next, select tools that you are comfortable with to store and analyze the data. Create a pattern of behavior in which you automatically add new customer information each and every time you receive it. Do something with the data. The more you use it, the more profitable you will find it.

Chapter 6

TARGET MARKETING

Deborah L. Owens and Cathy L. Martin

> Consumers now want to deal with the brands they like and the type of content they are interested in—on their own terms.
> —Matt McQueen, experience planning director,
> Arc Worldwide Publicity

A successful direct marketing strategy involves focused, targeted communications with potential or existing customers. The very nature of direct marketing suggests that it is driven by the needs of customers. Direct marketing goes beyond traditional market segmentation, to target micromarkets and individual markets tailored to the idiosyncrasies of each customer. Today's technology allows companies, large and small, to direct marketing efforts aimed at the individual market: the customer.

"The evolution from mass to micromarketing is a fundamental change driven as much by necessity as opportunity."[1] Direct marketing, when done correctly, is welcomed, personal, and relevant. As noted by Andrew Nibley, president and CEO of Marsteller, "We are now in a different world, where technology puts consumers in control."[2] Today's technology allows consumers to watch commercial-free programming, if they choose. Through technology such as digital video recorders, on-demand cable, and next-day $1.99 downloads of prime time shows, consumers choose what to watch, and when, without commercial interruptions. This chapter will outline various concepts, tools, and techniques that firms can use to target current and new customers to effectively compete in this new world of direct marketing.

CUSTOMERIZATION

Inherent within the concept of marketing is the ability to meet the needs and wants of customers. Direct marketing strategy when paired with technology allows for customization of the marketing message and medium. Hence the term "customerization," which suggests the convergence of customer needs with customization of the marketing message and medium. Technology today allows companies small and large to execute strategies for "customerization." Today's customers demand personalized approaches that meet their perceived unique needs and interests, while eschewing traditional approaches that treat them as one of the masses. For example, using tools no more sophisticated than Microsoft's Word, Excel, and Access programs an Avon representative can send a customized follow-up letter thanking a customer for the phone order on Wednesday, April 10, for the new spring lipstick shade, "Morning Dew," and matching nail polish, which will be delivered on April 17. Larger firms can utilize barcode scans of purchases, and frequent shopper card information to customize follow-up messages and create meaningful customer relationships.

In the distant past, small towns throughout the country were populated by shop owners that specialized in a line of merchandise such as ladies clothing, men's hats, or custom meats. In this scenario, Bob the Butcher knew that the banker's wife Barbara liked her pork chops sliced thickly and that the mayor's wife Mary liked her chops sliced thin. This specialized approach may not be familiar to many of today's consumers who are more accustomed to dealing with companies that try to be all things to all people, and chase after the elusive goal of increased market share. Characteristics of this micromarketing strategy include the following:

- More direct approach
- More individualized messages
- Highly interactive

Customerization is the means for reaching micromarkets and companies that are working under the old mass marketing paradigm will consistently lose ground to those firms that have recognized the creative power of linking customer's individualized needs to marketing efforts. Despite concerns that the new media age has made it more difficult for marketers to reach consumers, some industry executives see major benefits. Craig Leddy, senior analyst at Points North group consulting, in Larchmont, New York, sees this new landscape as ideal for direct marketers, "the relationship that advertisers can have with the consumer on portable [MP3] devices is more personal because it's on a little device being carried around, ... it's content the consumers choose to download."[3]

HISTORIC TRENDS IN TARGETING

It is insightful to consider the past, present, and future trends in targeting strategy. Customers are increasingly sophisticated and demanding. In the past, companies could achieve a competitive advantage simply by shifting from a mass-marketed, one-stop-shopping, we-know-you-all-like-it-this-way approach to a differentiated approach. An example of this would include the hotel industry's shift to differentiation.

For example, Marriott hotels increasingly differentiated their offerings to appeal to distinct target markets. Under this differentiated approach, Marriott offers multiple product offerings to appeal to distinct targeted customer groups. The Marriott Hotels and Resorts brand, is known for its high level of comprehensive services, offering business centers, concierge, and room service. The JW Marriott brand offers an even higher level of sophisticated service, with "a new dimension of luxury in a hotel with exquisite architectural detail, [and] the finest dining." Targeting yet a different group, Courtyard by Marriott is a hotel that caters to the needs of business travelers, providing high-speed Internet access, ergonomic work space, and a hot and fast breakfast buffet. In a distinctly different target segment is Residence Inn by Marriott, which is targeted to travelers who desire a home-like atmosphere. Complete with full kitchens, complimentary hot breakfasts, and evening social hours, Residence Inn meets the needs of travelers who wish to have a non-hotel-like atmosphere with a warm socially integrated atmosphere. To target the value-conscious consumer, Marriott offers Fairfield Inn. Fairfield Inn is bright and clean, and offers guests Marriott quality at an affordable price.[4]

Marriott's differentiated approach worked well in the past, but as in most industries, customers today want more personalization to meet their specific needs. As a result, Marriott has recently embraced micromarketing and more individualized approaches to develop targeted messages focused on the specific needs of customers. This more individualized approach, which will be discussed later in this chapter, allows customers to determine which promotional messages they will receive and how they would like to receive them.

Table 6-1 briefly summarizes the historic shift in targeting strategy. This historic shift is probably most directly observable in the retail grocery trade.[5] In the mass marketing era, grocery store chains targeted the mass market, using print and television advertising with one loud and consistent message: "lowest prices," "freshest produce," and "one-stop shopping." It was common in this era, which lasted up to the 1980s, for 80 percent of marketing expenditures to be spent on mass media.[6]

In the market segmentation era, grocery chains defined and segmented their market based on geographic terms, such as "the west coast market," "the Colorado market," or "the Los Angeles market." As noted by McCann,

> Although states and cities do exist as political entities and as places on a map, they are really just collections of people, stores, and other institutions. Marketing actions occur ... when the buyer and seller interact. These transactions are the outcomes of the marketing processes and data that moves marketing managers closer to the transactions are better than those that keep marketers in the fog by aggregating the data to levels that are not real markets.[7]

In the segmentation era, marketers saw the store as the real market and, hence, shifted their targeting to the store level, as scanner technology allowed brand managers and stores to assess the impact of in-store merchandising and sales promotions for product lines at the store level. In the segmentation era, with stores defined to be the real markets, brand resources were shifted to the store level, with a dramatic shift in marketing dollars from mass market advertising to sales promotions at the store level. Targeting at the store level increased as marketers realized that brand awareness was no longer sufficient. Marketing managers realized the inherent

Table 6-1 Historical Perspectives—Targeting Strategies

	Past **1950–1980**	**Present** **1980–2005**	**Future** **2006–**
Approach	Mass marketing	Market segmentation	Micromarkets
Message	One consistent	Multiple distinct	Individualized
Methods	Advertising	Sales promotion	Database methods
Interactivity	None	Limited	Optional
Measurability	None	Limited	Direct

power of the distribution channel to control what would or would not happen with their brands at the retail level.

Thus, beginning in the 1990s, marketing dollars shifted from traditional consumer-oriented advertising to sales promotion and incentives targeted at the channel members. Incentives were targeted at the wholesalers, distributors, and retailers who controlled the distribution system.

Promotion became king, as technology allowed tracking of return on the investment of the sales promotion, an accountability piece not present in traditional advertising.[8] Micromarketing goes one step beyond segmentation at the store level and targets individual customers. With the dominant use of credit or debit cards and UPC scanner technology, stores and brand managers have the name, address, and shopping patterns of most of their customers. With knowledge of each shopper's basket in a customer database segmenting at the customer level becomes possible. By looking at what is in their customers' shopping basket database, marketers can understand and get to know each customer, their preferences, and lifestyles. Unfortunately, too few retailers perform targeting at the customer level, preferring instead to build up store traffic by sales promotion at the store level (for example, 15 percent off all purchases) or at the brand level (for example, buy three get one free Stouffer's dinner).

Progressive marketers realize that technology allows them to target the individualized needs of their customers to create more personalized relationships. By mining the current customer database, companies can develop customized messages that demonstrate an appreciation of their customers in a very segmented and direct fashion. For example, contrast these two situations. In one hypothetical instance, a large grocery chain utilized an undifferentiated approach, offering a free turkey to all customers who spent $300 or more in November. In one actual instance, a small 16-store regional grocery chain decided to recognize their most loyal (and lucrative) customers by sorting their market by zip code and sending their best customers in each region an elegant arrangement of fall flowers, with the following note:

> In recognition of your very loyal patronage, we are sending you this autumn flower arrangement prepared especially for you. Please enjoy it with our complements. We never take your business for granted, as we know you have many options for grocery shopping. Thank you again for your business. Mr. John Doe, Store Manager.[9]

Utilizing existing technology to merge customer demographic information from loyalty cards, invoice records, or scanner data with customer purchase data allows all firms to create direct, highly interactive, and personalized approaches to recognize and reward the most loyal, profitable, and best customers. In addition, the "wow" value created by these more personalized approaches creates talk value, in the form of positive word-of-mouth that extends the reach and impact of microsegmentation strategies.

Consider that in far too many cases, the traditional marketing approaches reward not the best customers but those that are least profitable. Most grocery stores, for example, have special checkout lanes for customers with 10 items or less. Wouldn't it make more sense to have special lanes for those customers who are spending more than $200 per trip? Many mobile phone companies offer special introductory rates for the purchase of a new phone. In almost all cases these special promotions are only available to new subscribers. Instead, why not offer special discounts based on how long a customer has stayed with the company? Under this more individualized approach, customers who have been with the service provider for five years or more would get better promotional pricing to reward their loyalty. This type of tiered pricing could be justified on the basis of less paperwork, and lower overhead and processing costs, over the life of the account.

Targeting and delighting the firm's most loyal customer through a special recognition program is one small way to implement a micromarketing program. Instead, most grocery managers think that they are building customer loyalty when Ms. Jones presents her frequent shopper card, which is often mistakenly referred to as a loyalty card. Frequent shopper cards are rarely, if ever, appropriately used to actually build customer loyalty because most do not distinguish between the deal finder who shops wherever soda pop is cheapest that week, and the very loyal shopper who shops exclusively at one store, because of its high-quality produce and the friendly butcher who cuts the pork chops just the way Ms. Ledbetter likes them.

Targeting through sales promotion is a natural complement to a direct marketing campaign because of the direct feedback and inherent accountability. This shift, which began in the early 1990s continues today. For example, for roughly half the amount of a 30-second Super Bowl Ad, a newspaper delivered insert will target 55 million households with a four-color, full-page advertisement and a coupon that can be directly tied to a particular geographic region, store, and individual customer. In the segmentation era, the store was the target and store-stocking decisions could be customized to meet the needs of the area, be it a larger organic produce section, a sophisticated selection of upscale wines and spirits, or an expanded prepared foods area.

TARGETING THROUGH OPT-IN

One of the most successful strategies for targeting is the use of opt-in strategies. In an opt-in strategy, customers self-select whether they want to be part of your e-mail list or traditional mail directory. This form of message opt-in has also been referred to as "permission marketing." Permission or opt-in marketing can be as simple as a local dry cleaner asking customers whether they wish to be placed on their e-mail lists to receive notification of current promotional specials. For example, Fussy Cleaners, a regional dry cleaner in Ohio, asks customers to throw their business cards into a jar and promises, in return, to draw one card each week for a special "free dry cleaning service" and to notify them of upcoming shirt and dry cleaning specials. Likewise, Marriott Hotels may ask a hotel guest, upon checkout, to list their preferred e-mail address if they would like to receive information on upcoming special promotions and weekend offers.

Known in the field as an organic list, because they are home-grown, organic e-mail lists are an excellent method for targeting, because of their low cost and high return, and their ability to deliver one-to-one messages that are welcomed and sought after by the customer. These in-house created lists are developed from known prospects and established clients or are a cross-pollination from similarly minded businesses. In an organic list, the customer has given the firm specific permission to make a marketing contact. According to Morgan Stewart, director of strategic services for Indianapolis-based ExactTarget, permission-based organic lists are the most effective, which may account for their 38 percent annual net growth.[10] Stewart notes, "We need to get opt-in from customers and build a loyal base."

Microtargeting by opt-in has several unique advantages:

- Customers self qualify—It is no longer necessary to forecast the demographic criteria for qualification
- Customers are more welcoming to messages that they have "requested"—Higher response rates will be generated because of higher involvement
- Opt-in creates a customer relationship—Customer loyalty is a byproduct of enhanced customer relationships

- Eliminates the need and costs of rented e-mail lists—Rented e-mail lists may turn off prospects who are increasingly frustrated by phishing scares and unethical practices

In another example, Harvey Nelson, cofounder of Main Street Gourmet, a supplier of premixed muffin mix, cookie dough, and other specialty desserts to the restaurant and bakery industry, annually attends the National Restaurant Association Trade Show. This venue allows Main Street Gourmet to showcase new products such as their expanded Isabella's line of all-natural and healthy muffin and granola products. At the trade show, Main Street Gourmet asks potential customers what information they would like and in what format they would prefer to receive it. For example, some may wish to receive only information about certain categories of new products, such as upscale desserts, while others may want only information on healthy dessert options. Customers may elect to have updates on new products, promotions, or packaging sent via e-mail, Web site, mail, or fax, and they can also choose how frequently these updates are delivered.[11]

TARGETING WITH RSS: REALLY SIMPLE SYNDICATION

Targeting through opt-in can be achieved at a much more sophisticated level as well. Really Simple Syndication (RSS) is embraced by the technology-savvy, Generation Y and Millennial consumers. These consumers are part of the "find-it-for-me" generation in which consumers opt-in to have selected information "pushed" or sent to them. This may include news summaries on selected topics (for example, out-sourcing), specific product information (such as travel to Padre Island), or new spring fashion trends, with embedded Web links specific to the needs of the individual. One such proprietary product is RSSDirect from e-mail service provider Silverpop.[12]

For example, using the RSSDirect technology, GSG Entertainment, a music marketing company, used an opt-in format and RSS technology to generate individualized content based on consumer interests and their fan profiles, which made connections between like-minded music fans to exchange communications and share information about their favorite artists. The RSS technology allowed GSG Entertainment to effectively talk on a one-to-one basis with their targeted customers, while measuring feedback and sales generated.[13]

Returning to our travel industry example, Marriott Hotels has recently introduced RSS technology to its Web site. The Marriott Web site promotes Marriott eBreaks via RSS as follows:

RSS is simple, really. It stands for "Really Simple Syndication." With RSS, great travel deals come to you, not the other way around. Each week, eBreaks via RSS brings you the hottest deals all in one place. Convenient links allow you to learn more or book a stay whenever a deal appeals.[14]

RSS is growing in popularity with both customers and firms. For a summary of the key aspects of RSS technology, refer to Figure 6-1.

Figure 6-1 RSS Technology: Questions and Answers

Q: What is RSS technology?
A: **R**eally **S**imple **S**yndication or **R**ich **S**ite **S**ummary

Q: What is the purpose?
A: To distribute desired web based content to users; originally news headlines

Q: What are the benefits to consumers?
A: Desired content is in one central location for easy access, reducing the need for browsing for relevant articles or information.

Q: *What are the benefits for firms?*
A: It is a low cost and easy method to promote a web site, announce new products, or upcoming events.

Q: What format is it in?
A: While originally in RDF format; it is now in XML format

Q: What are its uses?
A: While first developed for news headlines, it is used to distribute any updated content such as new auction listing for a particular item, updated housing listings in a particular price range or area, or new entertainment options, or pricing data.

Q: What do I need to get started?
A: **Step 1:** Download Software. a free RSS newsreader or aggregator Examples BlogExpress, FeedReader or SharpReader (http://channels.lockergnome.com/rss/resources/)
Step 2: Got to your favorite websites. Most Websites have a list of links for RSS feed, that lets consumers select the topics they are interested in, and copy and past links to an RSS reader. Some RSS reader software can be set to autoselect RSS feeds, that you might be interested in, based on your browsing patterns,
Step 3: View the content. Many RSS Readers allow consumers to tailor how they prefer to see information, including the priority, and number of items.

Some portions adapted from ://www.rss-specifications.com/what-is-rss.htm and
http://channels.lockergnome.com/rss/resources/articles/quickstart.phtml (accessed on August 1, 2006).

TARGETING THE TOP

> Companies have to develop closer relationships with current
> customers.
> —Jay Conrad Levinson, former senior vice president,
> J. Walter Thompson, and author of *Guerrilla Marketing*

Targeting the top means targeting those customers who have the
greatest probability of using your products, services, and brand. The
trick has always been knowing how to identify these prospects. What
demographic and lifestyle group do they belong to? Historically targeting was aimed at identifying the income, age, geographic region,
and the activities, interests, and opinions of those thought to be in
the targeted segment. Marketing research was promoted as the
means to accomplish this task, and the purchase of customer lists
became the vehicle for executing the marketing strategy.

So what is the best target for your brand? The best target for
your existing product lines, and your newest product, are those customers who are already happy and loyal to your existing products.
Therefore, the most likely targets for your new product are those
customers that are now using products from your firm or its subsid-
iaries. While this may seem like a no-brainer, it is amazing how
many firms do not tap into the potential for targeting at the top. Jay
Levinson notes that one of the main tenets of effective marketing is
"increased transactions with existing customers rather concentrating
on getting new customers."[15] According to Levinson, the majority of
business lost is due to customers being ignored, and hence it is important to develop, cultivate, and direct significant attention to your
primary target: your existing customer base.

In an age of technology, there is no excuse not to cultivate your
existing customer base. Database technology, such as Microsoft
Access, allows even small businesses to identify and rank existing
customers by their contribution to profits. Rank ordering existing
customers by their level of profitability, not just sales, allows microtargeting strategies to be tailored to customers based on their direct
impact on the firm's bottom line. A distributor of medical supplies to
orthopedic practices, clinics, and hospitals utilized this approach
and found that less than 15 percent of the customers accounted for
more than 80 percent of profits. The sales force then targeted these
key accounts to better identify their needs and opportunities for
additional sales. Through developing more personalized relationships with these key accounts, the firm was able to generate additional profitable sales, reinforce loyalty, and leverage existing
accounts. In addition the return on the investments of the sales

force, time spent on theses targeted accounts was significantly higher than prospecting new accounts, no matter how sophisticated the segmentation strategy.

As another example, the Professional Golfers Association used a series of personalized targeted e-mails and postcard drops to past show attendees in an effort to boost attendance at their January 26–29, 2006, PGA Merchandise Show and Conference in Orlando, Florida. Based on the degree of past loyalty and their areas of interest, the targeted consumer received a series of contacts, including four e-mails, three postcards, and one brochure. This more personalized approach utilized the past attendees name and a customized message, such as "John Jones, you've been a loyal attendee at the PGA Show in Orlando and I want to recognize your support by personally inviting you to this year's show." The individualized communication also included a message based on the customer's area of interest, such as new instructional strategies for golf professionals, and information on new clothing trends for those involved with merchandising (such as buyers and managers of golf shops). In the future, Ed Several, vice president and general manager of PGA Golf Exhibitions, hopes to increase customization and implement more two-way communication, allowing attendees to select the type of information they would like to receive, resulting in more of a "me-based" approach.[16]

TARGETING THE eFLUENTIALS

When targeting the top, it is important to pay particular attention to the group of consumers who can be identified as eFluential. eFluentials are those consumers who are the market mavens of the new Web-based world.[17] This will be particularly important for Generation Y consumers, who will soon have the largest influence on spending. These are the children of the Baby Boomers, and they will soon exceed their parents both in sheer size and influence.[18] Referred to as Generation Y, Echo Boomers, or the Millennium Generation, these technologically sophisticated consumers, born between 1979 and 1994, are 60 million strong. Almost three times the size of Generation X, their influence on what is cool and what is not, what is in and what is not, will be dramatic.

This new demographic group wants to control not only their music and media viewing, (watch what we want, how we want, and where we want), but increasingly the advertising itself. The proliferation of inexpensive digital cameras, powerful computers, and off-the-shelf editing software can turn any 16 year old into a director.

Several companies have developed innovative targeting strategies by tapping into the eFluential group to design their ad content in a creative fashion. Targeting the creative segment of Generation Y, companies such as Nike-owned Converse, MasterCard, and L'Oreal are sponsoring "you-make-the-commercial contests" to have this influential group of consumers actually direct, produce, and develop their ad campaigns. For example, L'Oreal Paris is sponsoring a you-make-the-commercial contest on the teen entertainment site Varsity World.com. The winning entry of that contest was a video called "Juicy," made by two students at Granite Bay High School in California. In it, a young woman's lips and love life become more colorful when she puts on L'Oreal lip gloss."[19]

According to Andrew Nibley, the key characteristics of the eFluential group include those noted in Table 6-2. As studied by Roper ASW, since the 1940s these consumers have been the socially integrated new product adopters. The difference is that rather than talking to a small group of friends, through the Internet, on their Facebook, and in their My Space accounts, they can now communicate with literally hundreds of people instantaneously and influence thousands in a matter of minutes through their extensive and interlocking social networks. This ability to target this key group of eFluentials is critical to being able to leverage your brand in a positive and cost-effective fashion. It is critical that firms identify these eFluentials and then interact with them to address their concerns. If your product is great, they will tell people about it and if they have a negative product experience they will share that as well. This was the case of a college student, Rachel Fink, sharing with her extensive 300-member online social community of friends the positive experience she had with LastMinuteDeals.com,[20] as well as the negative experience she had getting service for her Mazda 6. Companies must target these

Table 6-2 Characteristics of eFluentials

Make friends online
Send e-mail messages to friends
Use Instant messaging
Post to news groups
Provide Feedback to Web sites
Participate in chat rooms
Write to politicians
Post messages to bulletin boards
Have a profile on Facebook or MySpace

---

consumers through their Customer Relationship Management (CRM) systems to effectively interact with those who had a great experience, but most importantly with those who did not.

TARGETING THROUGH CROSS-SELLING

> cross-sell (n): to seize the opportunity presented by a recent purchase in order to generate additional sales, often involving a more comprehensive solution to the customer's needs.
> —www.nimblefish.com/html/solutions_crosssell.html

One of the major shifts in consumers today is their desire to not be marketed to. Consumers today prefer more subtle contacts that seemingly understand who they are and what they are about. Andrew Nibley, CEO of Marsteller, explains that this is particularly true for Generation Y consumers, who are very adept at media meshing and for whom cross-selling may be particularly effective. Media meshing is the desire for consumers to have messages that are targeted at them delivered through a variety of mediums and sources. The new consumer wants to enhance their experience by accessing multiple media at the same time. This group of consumers may be watching "American Idol" on their television, while voting for their favorite contestant on their laptop, posting a comment on their "Facebook" wall, and sending a text message to a friend to ask them who they voted for. These consumers enjoy multitasking using alternative mediums and thrive on two-way interactivity.[21]

Table 6-3 offers some examples of cross-selling. According to Nibley, this group of Millennial consumers is ideal for cross-selling, because they often define themselves through the brands they purchase. These consumers want transparency and honesty when targeted to. The Millennial Generation of consumers may define themselves as an "Apple Person," a "Nike Person," or a "Baby Phat" person. These consumers do not mind being targeted to if they perceive that it is relevant to their interests and concerns. They want to be in control and interact with the brands that define them.

TARGETING THROUGH CO-MARKETING

Co-marketing is an effective vehicle for targeting customers who have related areas of interest. Strategic partnerships or loose alliances have proven very successful for both well-known and emerging brands. From a targeting perspective, firms can leverage

Table 6-3 Examples of Cross-Selling

Firm	Current Products	Potential Cross-Product Targeting
Lands' End	Children's clothing	Home goods/bedding
Advanced Elastomer	Santoprene	Nylon bondable Santoprene systems
HP	Printers	Digital picture printing kiosks
Apple Computer	iPods	Computers (laptops and desktops)
Baby Phat	Trendy jeans	Beauty products and lingerie

their existing customers with noncompeting businesses and obtain access to customers that may not otherwise be efficiently targeted. In addition, a firm can share ad and promotional costs. Co-marketing alliances between such well-known firms demonstrate the use of co-marketing as a targeting tool. For example, to help celebrate their 100th year anniversary of the birth of its founder, Walt Disney, Walt Disney World developed a $250 million advertising and promotion campaign utilizing a co-marketing alliance, coupled with a strong Web-based presence on DisneyWorld.com to target customers, with the aim of boosting attendance at their theme parks. The advertising campaign utilized a synergistic strategy targeting the existing customers of such well-known brands as McDonald's Corp., Walt Disney. Coca-Cola Co., Kellogg's Co., and Hallmark Cards. Disney had identified their distinct core customer segments as families, empty nesters, tweens, and grandparents.[22] More creative approaches to co-marketing are also possible. ESPN targeted their sports-minded fans through the placement of the ESPN brand in movies. Starting with the film "Mr. 3000," in which the lead female was an ESPN Reporter, and continuing to the film "Dodgeball," in which the final game is covered by a fictional station "ESPN 8: The Ocho," this success was followed by inserts in the playful film "Herbie: Fully Loaded," and the remake of the action sports dramas "The Longest Yard" with Adam Sandler. ESPN did not pay for the placement but did it to extend their brand.[23] In each of these cases, co-marketing alliances were used as a means to leverage resources and target customers who had already shown an interest in a particular product or service. In the case of ESPN's placement in the sports- and action-oriented movies, the customers attending the movie had already shown an interest in the sports field, which created an ideal targeting opportunity for ESPN. When selecting partners for co-alliances for direct marketing remember the following: *What you can measure you can manage.*

Targeting at the customer level is best not only for reaching the customer, but also for managing the marketing process. Direct marketing allows for measuring the effectiveness of each strategic action not at some meaningless measure of aggregation (for example, the number of tickets sold in Des Moines) but at the individual customer level. Season ticket subscribers to a regional playhouse could be targeted based on the number of years that they have subscribed. Subscribers for three or more years could be provided with a complimentary drink ticket for the first performance of the season. Those that have subscribed for at least five years could be awarded free parking to recognize their loyalty. Those that had previously upgraded to better seats could be thanked for their patronage and rewarded with a preperformance cocktail reception. The impact of these efforts can be directly measured and benchmarked against previous years to evaluate the return on these targeted marketing efforts.

A NEW AGE

Guess what? We have lost control!
—Andrew Nibley, president and CEO, Marsteller, and
former CEO, rollingstone.com

This is indeed a new age of targeting. An age in which marketers can no longer treat everyone the same. It is an age in which each consumer wants to be treated as an individual. As noted by William Cron, marketing professor, Southern Methodist University, and a former brand manager for Proctor & Gamble, "Increasingly, I'm finding that I'm having to throw out everything that I have learned. Marketing is going to one-on-one, co-hort and experiential marketing."[24]

Chapter 7

DIFFERENTIATING AND POSITIONING: FORMULATING AND IMPLEMENTING THE RIGHT STRATEGIES

Dale M. Lewison

> If you don't know where you are going, any road will take you there.
>
> —Koran

A direct marketer uses strategy to chart a course of action, giving focus for all of the firm's efforts. Strategy can be the realization of a corporate vision, the completion of a business mission, and/or the attainment of a marketing goal. Strategy can provide your firm with an identity—who you are and what you do. Strategy also simplifies and explains the direct marketer's business intentions and activities concisely and meaningfully. Finally, strategy may be directed at finding the right match between the firm's internal capabilities and its external opportunities.

Strategy took a new gadget, the laptop computer, and carried it from the hands of techno geeks into posh leather bags carried by millions of business people. The business office is now anywhere you want to be, from the beach to the airport. Few things in life happen completely by accident. Yes, we all hear stories like that of 3M and Post-it Notes. Wouldn't it be nice if we could all stumble on a similar accident? However, many times, like laptop computers and Post-it Notes, a discovery is made through a new technological break-through, a chance discovery or accident, or through a seemingly "crazy" idea from an "entrepreneur." Yet, beyond the level of innovation, once you actually have an idea, you must have a clear, well thought out path to lead to your success. Even Post-it Notes eventually had to have a marketing strategy.

Differentiating and positioning strategies are two means by which you can structure your company's offer. Consumers think in relative terms; they organize their world by making comparisons between various elements within their environment. If you hear V-8, you might think quality tomato juice, whereas someone else might think automobile engine.

An offer needs to be better, cheaper, quicker, easier, stronger, newer, or more convenient to communicate any advantage your product or service has over another.

UNDERSTANDING DIFFERENTIATION

Differentiation is the approach of developing a set of unique and meaningful "points of difference" that are capable of distinguishing your offer from that of your competitors and that give it differential advantage. In simple terms, why would a customer buy from you instead of your competition?

For example, you might think you know what quality is, but it should never be assumed. Quality is what your targeted customer says it is; frequently it is not what the marketer thinks it is or wants it to be. To find out what quality is, ask the customer. A customer-centric definition of quality is that it is the ability of the good to

Figure 7-1 Strategy Formulation Process

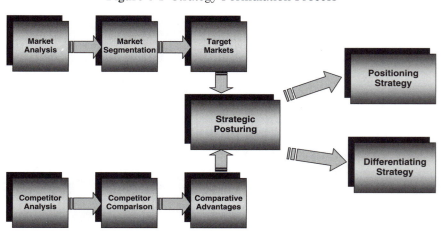

match or exceed the customer's performance expectations. The importance of quality is that it determines to what extent the good's functional features are able to perform the functions that it was designed to perform. From the customer perspective of quality, the question is, "What will it do for me?"

Consumers want reliability, which relates to the length of time it takes for a failure or malfunction to occur. How long should your lawn mower run before it won't start one early spring morning? Consumers want conformance, which is the expectation that the good conforms to the materials and workmanship quoted for the product. If it says stainless steel, then it should be stainless steel. These are the "quality killers."

The Importance of the Brand

A brand is a name, term, phrase, symbol, design, or any other feature used to identify and represent a good and the direct marketer who sells it. Brands are absolutely vital to the goods differentiation

Figure 7-2 Quality Dimensions

process. To be successful, you need to progress through three stages—brand recognition, brand image, and brand loyalty—to build brand equity (the total world or strength of the brand in the marketplace). Strong brand equity is a clear indicator of your success at differentiating.

Do customers recognize you? Do you have brand recognition? Before customers can compare your offering with those of other firms, they must first be aware of both offerings and have the means to make a comparison. You can use a wide variety of channels of communication (print, broadcast, telephone, Internet, and fax) to gain exposure and build awareness. This is the first stage.

Cultivating a brand image is critical. In this second stage of the differentiation process, you need to construct a viable and compelling image (personality, aura, impression, or feeling) of the good, which has the ability to attract and hold the attention of the consumer. Brand image represents the symbolic value of the good in the eyes of consumers and how they feel about the merits of your good relative to the merits of the competition. Image is concerned with emotional differentiation. Although we don't want to admit it, we almost always buy emotionally and defend logically. So, you can attract customers to buy your product through brand equity, but to hang on to them long term and generate word of mouth, you also must have the quality and performance.

Further enhancement of brand acceptance is achieved when you are able to upgrade the customer to being brand loyal—in other words, your good is favored among other choices. Brand loyalty comes in degrees. There is brand preference, a limited degree of loyalty in which the customer will choose a brand if it is readily available (the *Wall Street Journal* sends a renewal notice before subscription expiration). If the preferred brand is not available, customers may choose something else—known as brand switching. The ultimate degree of brand loyalty is brand insistence—your customer will not accept substitutes for your product. Brand insistence is almost never achieved. Usually brand loyalty is a lofty goal. Brand insistence is usually reserved for luxury products like Louis Vuitton purses. A consumer doesn't go out and buy a Louis Vuitton handbag because they desperately need a handbag; they want it because it's Louis Vuitton.

Service Actions

Customer service actions mean how customer services are performed and the way in which customers are treated, assisted, and served. Well-treated customers are loyal ones. Harley Davidson has effectively built strong loyalties among its buyers by making them HOGs—members of the Harley Owners Group. Using a multichannel direct marketing approach, group members have created a cult brand by organizing rides, sponsoring training courses, holding local and national social events, and supporting charity fundraisers. You can use technology and relationship-building tactics to become time-lier, convenient, faster, friendlier, and more concerned, adaptive, attentive, and professional. Competence, courtesy, credibility, will-ingness, responsiveness, reliability, and communication skills are all essential attributes of a well-planned and executed differentiation strategy.

Price Differentiation

Price decisions can help you promote customer awareness and direct customer attention toward value. The right price is a competi-tive price—one that is set in relation to the competition. In using a competition-based pricing scheme to differentiate the direct market-ing offer, your alternatives are below-market, at-market, and above-market pricing.

You can undersell the competitors by selling below the going or traditional market price. Being different is being cheaper. Being rec-ognized as the below-market competitor necessitates tighter controls and managed cost structures. You must pursue an ongoing strategy of continuous improvement in operational efficiency and effective-ness to continue along this path. Wal-Mart has become the world's largest retailer by pursuing a price leadership strategy. To support its promotions of continuously falling prices, the firm practices the mantra of selling their products at the lowest possible price, sup-ported by continuous improvement in operational efficiency and effectiveness.

In pursuing an at-market pricing scheme, you are electing to deemphasize price and instead emphasize nonprice elements of the total offer as your focus of differentiation. Being stuck in the middle means that there is no noticeable difference that might distinguish you from the me-too crowd of indifference. J.C. Penney hopes it can bring growth to the tired section of the retail world—the middle-market department store—by developing private labels that target conservative, traditional, modern, or trendy women's clothing. Penney's is repositioning itself away from conservative and tradi-tional to fashions that reflect a more modern and trendy look—flying in the face of conventional retailing wisdom that states that the best positioning strategy of growth exists at the discount end of the market (Wal-Mart, Target, Kohl's) or the high-end market (Nordstrom and Neiman Marcus).

In above-market pricing, you set prices at levels that are significantly higher than average markets. To justify these prices, you must carefully communicate to the customer what extra benefits they can expect to receive for paying higher prices. Do you offer extras such as better quality goods, higher service levels, greater service support, more exclusive merchandise, improved customer conveniences, more personalized attention, or any other benefit that would enhance the customer's enjoyment in your product? Some middle- and upper-income mothers are more style and brand conscious than other parenting segments. Often referred to as "yoga mamas," this consumer segment is willing to spend three times the price of popular mass brands to dress their children in organic cotton shirts and pajamas from niche marketers like Hanna Anderson and Mama's Earth and in Italian leather toddler shoes, and wheel them around in ergonomically designed Bugaboo strollers.

Product Leadership

Offering products and services that push performance boundaries through innovation and new developments requires leadership discipline. Product and service leadership requires you to focus on the core process of product invention and market exploitation and to be the kind of company that encourages experimentation and out-of-the-box thinking. In 2003, an innovative Infrared Heating Pad from Canada was introduced in the American market. The heating pad was not available in retail stores. Purchases could only be made through direct mail solicitations and via a newspaper advertising campaign. Although the heating pad was priced at $224 and regular heating pads retail for $29, the innovative technology behind the new device made it a best seller and a product leader.

Customer Intimacy

Customer intimacy differentiation stresses delivering what specific customers want by gaining intimate knowledge of them and their behaviors, and thus exceeding their expectations about the product or solution you deliver. Direct marketers attempt to optimize their results by empowering their employees who deal directly with the customer. Interactive Web sites that specialize in weight loss and dating relationships use an unprecedented degree of personalization to achieve high traffic and customer satisfaction.

POSITIONING APPROACHES

Positioning is the logical extension of differentiating. While being different is crucial to your success, positioning carries the competitive referencing strategy to the next level. Establishing a "place in the consumer's mind" is the underlying concept in the use of positioning. It's more than being different; it is about being more appropriate, more consistent, and more desirable when customers make direct comparisons and assessments.

Creative and Adaptive Approaches

There are two approaches—creative and adaptive. Creative positioning creates a new and different consumer perception of your offering to enhance the likelihood that some consumers will find your offer superior to the others. By using competitors as benchmarks or reference points, you can stress the relative advantages and attributes of your products and organizations. By controlling the "points of reference" that comprise a position, your firm selects points of reference that cast you and your programs in the most favorable light. It requires out-of-the-box thinking to find attributes that are new, different, and worthwhile.

Adaptive positioning, or repositioning, focuses on rearranging and changing ideas and associations that already exist in the consumer's mind and connecting them to your marketing programs. Changing consumer mind-sets after they have been established is usually a difficult task. To appeal to a broader market, Tiffany, the upscale jewelry retailer, has moved somewhat downscale by opening more stores at mall locations, selling over the Internet, and advertising a wider range of price points. This repositioning strategy is designed to build greater loyalty among existing customers and introduce themselves to those consumers who aspire to be Tiffany customers.[1]

Positioning Process

Positioning implementation places the most distinguishing ideas about your product, brand, or organization in the minds of consumers. The process of positioning is both an art and a science. In essence, you seek to understand how the offer can gain a more favorable market reception than those extended by competitors. Implementation of a positioning strategy can be accomplished by using the ABCs of positioning and several tactical actions that can be used to secure the desired consumer mind-set.

The identification of attributes (A) is the first step in the development of a positioning strategy. What characteristics distinguish your market offering from the competition? Product feature attributes like service levels, pricing points, promotional themes, distributor networks, and image factors may provide the basis for creating a distinctive position in the market. Ikea, the Swedish furniture and home products company, has become, in the words of one *Business Week* writer, "a global cult brand" by creating "a state of mind that revolves around contemporary design, low prices, wacky promotions, and an enthusiasm that few institutions in or out of business can muster.... Ikea provides a one-stop sanctuary for coolness. It is a trusted safe zone [for] a like-minded cost/design/environmentally sensitive global tribe."[2]

The second step in the positioning process is the delineation of benefits (B). Finding the comparative advantages of your offering is an essential goal. To qualify as a comparative advantage, it should deliver high value, deliver something different, deliver higher quality, promote ease of understanding, be difficult to copy, be affordable, and be profitable. Ford Motor Company markets its gas-electric Escape SUV as a full-fledged hybrid. Compared with previous hybrids on the market, the Escape hybrid offers the space, power, and rough-weather capability of an SUV while being environmentally friendly and more economic to operate.

The final step to building a successful market position is to communicate claims (C) and promises that clearly convey to your customers the best comparative position. Market positions are established by promoting the product, brand, or organization as being bigger, better, cheaper, faster, easier, newer, cooler, or some other descriptor of its advantages. Successful long-term market positioning campaigns must be based on claims that can be substantiated, otherwise it becomes all illusion and hype. VISA Signature credit card stakes its claim to exclusiveness and prestige. A tagline for one of its print ads claims, "Life takes pull—life takes VISA." Hard-to-get dinner reservations, VIP packages for choice sporting events, and complimentary concierge services are some of the benefits afforded to individuals who carry the VISA Signature card.

Because relatively few offers are totally superior to those of the competition, you need to carefully select dimensions that are both different and consequential. Some direct marketers like the one-benefit strategy while others believe that a multibenefit approach is better. The one-benefit strategy flows from the "unique selling proposition" (USP)—the belief that consumers better remember one message than many. Volvo positions its vehicles as superior in safety and durability following a dual-benefit strategy.

You can use many different tactics in the positioning process. Consider these tactics:

Quality positioning focuses on touting the superiority of a good or service using selected criteria. In its advertisement with the tagline "Refining a legacy," the copy of a Johnnie Walker ad describes its prize-winning standards for blended Blue Label scotch whiskey. The principal positioning claim is that skillful blending of several whiskeys creates a depth of flavor unattainable with a single-malt whiskey.

Image positioning attempts to create an attractive and motivating visual mind-set for the product. Porsche's tagline "A body built for sin" introduces the new Cayman S as a vehicle designed to stir things up. The copy supports the sensual image: "Seduction manifested in sheet metal. The unmistakable curve of its roofline arches, past taut, muscular hips. Yet beneath lies pure power."

Parentage positioning uses product lineage as a tool for positioning products and brands. Using a photo of the ancestors of the Mercedes Benz S class model, the car company's tagline reads, "Buying a car is like getting married. It's a good idea to know the family."

Value positioning has been at the core of Vanguard Funds since their inception. Advertisements publicize the firm's record: how a 30-year commitment to low-cost, long-term investing led to 90 percent of the firm's mutual funds outperforming their competitors. Investors are encouraged to the take the high road to low-cost investing.

Features positioning directs consumer attention toward specific physical design and material features. Asics' "Velostretch" top was designed to keep the body cool and dry by channeling airflow while stretching with every movement.

Fear positioning plays on consumer worries. Neutrogena's tagline "Protect your skin from daily cell damage" claims that its Healthy Defense daily moisturizer provides UV protection against sun damage and premature aging. Supporting this positioning strategy is the claim to being "No. 1 dermatologist recommended."

Channel positioning offers customers a choice. Eddie Bauer takes multichannel retailing beyond the channel mix of most of its competitors by enabling customers to purchase through direct-order channels (catalog, Internet, telephone) as well as in-store venues. The firm also allows customers to use direct-order kiosks in stores to search for products that are not in stock in the store but are available through its Web and catalog channels.

Relational positioning is at the heart of relationship marketing. Building and maintaining strong relationships is the core strategy in relational positioning. Credit Suisse uses the tagline "Some think competition. We think partnership." The investment firm attempts to build these relationships by serving as a catalyst to "bring together new partners to achieve results that can make the difference for our clients."

Aspiration positioning is concerned with goal achievement, future accomplishments, and getting the job done. ConocoPhillips tagline "What if everyone just settled for average?" promotes its aspirations of turning "what ifs" into "what's next." The crux of aspiration positioning is that high aspirations result in superior performance.

Solution positioning helps prospective customers with a problem by providing possible resolutions. Transamerica's tagline "I want my grandson to spend my money" addresses the issue of deciding who benefits from your success. Transamerica offers flexible solutions to insurance, investment, and retirement strategies that are consistent with their clients' wishes.

Rivalry-based positioning is epitomized by a Grey Goose Vodka promotion that claims it is the "No. 1 tasting vodka in the world." To support this positioning claim, the ad cites a blind taste test of more than 40 vodkas conducted by the Beverage Testing Institute of Chicago. Based on the criteria of smoothness, nose, and taste, Grey Goose received the top score of 96.

Emotional positioning shows concern for some special cause, public issue, charitable need, or personal concern. Toyota pledges, "Our vehicles don't just take people to work, they put people to work." Creating more U.S. jobs and cleaner U.S. plants, Toyota positions itself as a caring organization that is concerned about its employees and the environment.

Benefit positioning presents the prospective buyer with what the product can do for them. IBM, the world's largest technology and business consultancy, promotes its "On-Demand Business" service as a means of responding to the "pace, pressures, and fluctuations of the on-demand world. Assistance in rethinking processes, integrating operations, and identifying bottlenecks, blind spots, and inefficiencies are some ways in which clients can benefit.

Additional positioning tactics include price leadership (the lowest or the best), pioneer status (the newest or most innovative), focus (credibility that comes with product or market specialization), and category (insight that results from creating product categories and classifying the firm's products with regard to a favorable one).

SUMMARY

Differentiating and positioning strategies are the two means by which you can structure competitive marketing offerings. Differentiation is the marketing strategy of developing and marketing a set of unique and meaningful "points of difference" that are capable of distinguishing the direct marketer's offer from those of its competitors. Competitive advantages can be achieved by creating different and consequential offerings of goods, services, images, promotions, prices, and logistical opportunities for the direct interactive customer.

Below-, at-, and above-market prices are the three major alternatives that direct marketers can select to differentiate their offering on the basis of price. Different value disciplines (operating excellence, product leadership, and customer intimacy) demand different business models to be effective at differentiating direct marketing programs. Positioning is the logical extension of differentiating. Positioning is the marketing strategy in which a distinctive, meaningful, and interesting position is created for a direct marketing organization and its offering in the minds of a targeted group of consumers relative to their mind-sets for competing offers. Direct marketers approach positioning as either a problem of creating positioning (establishing a new and different consumer perception of the offer) or adaptive positioning (rearranging and changing ideas and associations that already exist in the consumer's mind and connect them in a positive way to the current offering). The ABCs of positioning is the way in which marketers identify attributes (A), delineate benefits (B), and communicate claims (C) as part of the overall process for implementing a positioning strategy. Specific tactics for implementing a positioning strategy include positioning on the bases of quality, image, parentage, value, features, fear, channels, relations, aspirations, price, problem solutions, competitive rivalry, emotions, and benefits.

Chapter 8

UNIQUE VALUE PROPOSITION: DEVELOPING AND IMPLEMENTING THE RIGHT OFFER

Dale M. Lewison and Mark Collins

People don't ask for facts in making up their minds. They would rather have one good, soul-satisfying emotion than a dozen facts.
                    —Robert Keith Leavitt, historian and author

Are you contacting customers in a variety of ways, trying to provide them with specialized information, all the while hoping for a sale? Then you are attempting direct marketing. And you probably already know something significant—you can't be all things to all customers.

To succeed, you must find the unique value that your firm alone can best deliver to a select—and profitable—group of customers. In the highly fragmented marketplace today, customer expectations are more demanding while their patronage is less loyal. Creating meaningful and useful customer value is all about what Peter Drucker describes as "doing the right things," as opposed to "doing things right." You already know that snazzy marketing efforts with flashy promotions simply cannot compete with solid offers that have attributes and benefits more highly prized than your own.

A persuasive offer speaks to the prospect's inner mind-set. Most consumers are skeptical about most offers. They remember Popeil's Pocket Fisherman and the Vegematic vegetable cutter. They've heard about Christmas bubble lights that leaked dangerous chemicals. They remember a boat load of product recalls over the years. Customers are even more cynical and doubtful about new offers from new sellers.

They are not willing to spend more time, money, or effort considering an offer that is not immediately clear and relevant. Your offer needs to communicate to the prospect that its attributes and benefits represent a significant "return on investment" for their time, money, and effort. Realistically, every offer must address the following questions that are being asked within the unspoken realm of the prospect's mind-set: (1) What exactly are you selling? (2) How much is it going to cost me? (3) Why should I trust you? and (4) Why should I buy? That is, what's in it for me? Offers that clearly communicate the answers to each of these questions have a much better chance to impact the customer's mind-set.

To create a value proposition, a six-step process for developing an offer will attract and hold the attention of consumers. The six steps are conceptualizing, targeting, creating, structuring, testing, and changing the offer. This process contributes to our discussion of how to create an offer that represents the most desirable value proposition in the eyes of the customer.

Figure 8-1 The Five-Step Process for Developing and Implementing Effective Value Offers

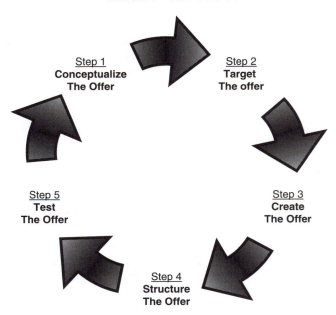

STEP 1: CONCEPTUALIZING THE OFFER

What is an offer? The offer that you will make is the sum total of all of the attributes and benefits that you are presenting to the consumer as an exchange proposal. Your offer is a contract, a deal, or a proposition that is designed to secure a favorable response. It is a combination of goods and services supported by a compelling mix of price, promotion, and channels, together with terms and condition of exchange.

The offer tells the customer what he gets and what he needs to do to get it. For example, if you fax me this order form to buy four cases of this widget by next Thursday, you get another 10 percent off. A good offer creates customer awareness, interest, and trial because they are cues to encourage customers to respond.

Direct marketing differs from traditional marketing, so it is important not to confuse the two. If a customer goes into a store to buy an iPod for her teenage son, she is ready to buy. When the typical direct marketing customer receives an offer, he or she may not be in the mood to buy right at that moment, so the direct marketing offer has a great burden to carry. The offer has to be better.

Some offers are obviously better than others. Why? There are some variables or benchmarks that can be used to ensure a better offer. You need not be overwhelmed by the number of variables. It would be impossible to follow them all, but these will provide you with some good starters:

- Importance. The key attributes and benefits of your offer should be effectively communicated—as you know, these are the offers that will make the consumer respond.

- Distinctiveness. Does your offer contain one or more "points of difference" that differentiates your offer from others? Blah-Blah Cellular Phone Company's offer includes more free minutes than anyone else, plus a free phone.

- Affordability. Is your offer consistent with the targeted consumer's ability to buy? The absolute price determines the affordability while the relative price determines the offer's competitiveness with others.

- Superiority. Does the offer contain one or more attributes that consumers will recognize and accept as being a cut above the others?

- Hard to Duplicate. Can competitors easily match the offer? If not, then your firm has a better and more sustainable advantage. A unique and distinctive offer has a longer life cycle.

- Beneficial. What specific benefits are contained in the offer? Are these important benefits for the customer? It should meet or exceed the customer's expectations.

- Compelling. Is the offer sufficient to ensure a customer reaction? What are the must haves in the viewpoint of the customer? A positive response from your customer is often the result of two or three top-perceived benefits.
- Tangibility. Can the customer see, smell, taste, or feel the benefits of the offer? If "seeing is believing," then your offer should appeal to the senses. A creative script, a realistic visual, and representative samples are but a few ways that the offer can be substantiated.
- Profitable. Will the offer be profitable? Will it generate an acceptable return? Are operating expenses manageable?

STEP 2: TARGETING THE OFFER

Successful offers are tailored offers targeted at specific consumers. The very nature and purpose of direct marketing is that this marketing venue allows the marketer to approach the consumer on a one-to-one basis. Using carefully constructed customer lists and databases, you can zero in on the specific needs of a select and targeted group of consumers.

STEP 3: CREATING THE OFFER

A useful tool for developing and communicating the offer as a value proposition is the value equation—an implied promise made by direct marketers to the customer that they will deliver a particular package of values that the consumer is seeking. Because value is in the eyes of the beholder, then it is the customer's own notion of what creates good value that should direct the development of the total offer.

Value is interactive and ever changing. It can be a function of one or more of the following: (1) product design, (2) product quality, (3) product mix, (4) product benefits, (5) pricing points, (6) supporting services, (7) promotional incentives, (8) risk reducers, and (9) terms and conditions. In short, value is simply giving customers what they want, when they want it, how they want it, at a price they consider fair.

Product Design

Product design encompasses the product's functional attributes and aesthetic features. Its attributes and features represent the tangible bundle of characteristics that describe what the product is and

Figure 8-2 The Components Comprising the Value Equation

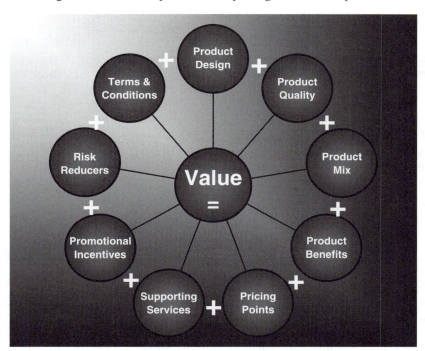

what it does. The functional attributes are the product's biological or chemical structure together with its physical design specifications, size, weight, and such. Can the product do what it was designed to perform? A personal data assistant (PDA) has specifications that determine what it can do and how fast. If the PDA does not have the functional performance the customer is seeking, none of the other considerations associated with the offer are relevant. Consider Aleve, an over-the-counter pain medication that is only taken every 8 to 12 hours. Users can go through the work day or the night without additional medication, a product feature that makes this product popular.

Aesthetic features are also important and appeal to the senses. Most consumers have a preconceived idea of what the product should be in an aesthetic sense. If the product does not match these notions, the offer will not be widely accepted. A direct marketer needs to find the means of effectively portraying the products with still photos using detailed angles and other visual representation of the product.

Product Quality

Can the product live up to the performance expectations of the consumer? The two central questions are (1) Do expected benefits equal realized benefits? and (2) Is the consumer's perceived value from the exchange process enhanced? Using better raw materials and craftsmanship improved the product. A more superior product has fewer defects or failures. Effective quality assurance controls can eliminate most of the defects through continuous improvement, even if achieving zero defects is not economically feasible. The use of testimonials and research study results are often used in direct marketing campaigns as surrogate evidence for good quality.

Product Mix

The product mix is the full range or composition of products that are offered. They should be constructed as "bundles of benefits" capable of satisfying the buyer. It can be a good, a service, or an idea. Products can be combined and classified in terms of (1) satisfying a particular need (health and beauty aids), (2) being used together (insurance and real estate services), (3) being purchased or used by the same customer group (steel or metals industry), and (4) marketing a vendor or manufacturer (Nike, Reebok, and Converse). Product items are specific products within a product line that are unique and distinguishable from other products within and outside the product line.

You, the direct marketer, must decide on the nature of the mix you offer, in terms of variety and assortment of products. Your strategy might involve only one or a few product lines or a wide variety. That will be your assortment. The promotional piece (package insert, statement stuffer, or co-op mailing) might have 1 item or 400 items. The product mix can be adjusted to create value offers.

Going from a narrow variety/shallow assortment, which is the most limited product selection (suited to one-to-one marketing), to the wide variety/shallow assortment (a little bit of everything), to the narrow variety/deep assortment (for a select group of customers), and finally to the wide variety/deep assortment (one-stop-shopping experience), there is room to modify and change the offer accordingly.

Product Benefits

The buyer or responder expects to benefit in some way from the purchase. The Bali minimizer bra promises to reduce the bust line by

Figure 8-3 The Four Basic Variety/Assortment Strategies

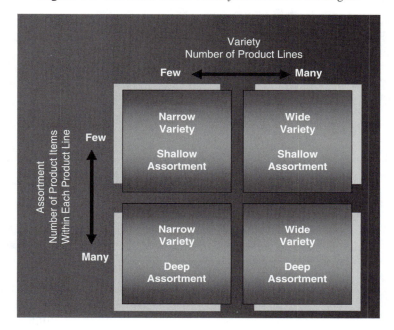

1³/₄ inches, making blouses and blazers fit much better. Buyers of any Lexus automobile at a Cleveland area dealer get free car washes on Saturdays. Who will they meet on Saturdays? Other Lexus owners.

There are operational benefits for the product. The product might clean, entertain, transport, process, cool, inform, analyze, light, teach, or problem solve. From the operational standpoint, people do not buy snow blowers; they buy clean driveways. Organizational buyers don't buy lubricants; they buy trouble-free operations, longer machine life, and better returns on the company's capital investments.

Pricing Points

The right price is the one for which the absolute price meets the buyer's value expectations of affordability and the relative price meets the buyer's perception of competitiveness. Price points are established using tactics, such as cost-based, customer-based, competition-based, vendor-based, differential, geographic, product-line, psychological, and promotional pricing.

- Cost-based pricing. To arrive at a cost-based price, you add a profit margin (dollar or percentage) to the cost of the product to arrive at a selling price.

- Customer-based pricing. The price must meet customer expectations. Perceived-value pricing involves setting the price based on the customer's perceptions and beliefs as to what the product is worth. Demand-backward pricing means that you start with a reliable estimate as to what the customer is willing to pay and work back by subtracting estimates of per-unit cost from the estimated per-unit selling price.

- Competition-based pricing. The seller sets prices in relation to the competition. Sometimes we might choose to simply add product lines that are both desirable and consistent with market leaders. Both Dyson and Hoover have chosen to create and market high-end vacuum cleaners that are priced competitively with Oreck. The tactics of below-, at-, and above-market pricing were discussed in chapter 7.

- Vendor-based pricing. Business-to-business pricing might take the form of vendor-based pricing—the practice of establishing a basic list price that is adjusted for each customer. Discounts and allowances may be given and are reductions from the price list.

- Differential pricing. Selling the same product to different markets at different times at different prices is differential pricing. Sellers use flexible pricing, periodic discounting, and random discounting as a way to take advantage of customer price sensitivity.

- Geographic pricing. You aren't located the same distance from your customers. Uniform delivery pricing involves the seller charging buyers regardless of their location. In zone pricing, all buyers in a certain area are in a single price zone. In basing-point pricing, pricing is designed to increase the geographic reach by designating a single basing point location (like Atlanta, St. Louis, or Portland) and charging all from where the shipment originated.

- Product-line pricing. Price bundling is marketing two or more goods or services in a single package for a special price. The seller hopes that by creating the package deal, he or she will generate profitable sales from current customers. McDonald's offers the "value meal," which is an example of price bundling. Captive pricing means selling the basic product item (Fusion razor) at a reduced price, but selling essential consumables (blades) at prices with higher margins. A mail order retailer might give away a free cubic zirconium and then offer to have it mounted at a price that produces sufficient margin to make the offer profitable. Concept selling means charging a higher price for a good or service but justifying the price by convincing the customer that the total benefits package is worth the deal. For example, a health club might package several goods and services into a "total wellness" offer of exercise, nutrition, and supplements. In price lining, several product items within a product line are grouped into a price zone (low/economical, average/family, prestige/luxury) and offer several price points within each price zone.

- Psychological pricing. Your offering is adapted to accommodate psychological influences like motivation, perception, learning, and attitudes on the buyer. We've all seen the $9.99 item—this results from the belief that consumers perceive odd prices as being lower than even numbers. Giving a discount for ordering more than one item is multiple pricing. Printers use this form of pricing regularly.

- Promotional pricing. In promotional prices, the prices are lowered to build sales, attract buyers, and create value. Leader prices are used for high-demand products at attractive prices. A low-leader is a reduction but will cover the cost of the goods sold and operating expenses. A loss-leader is a price below the seller's cost of good sold. If you use leader tactics, then it is usually to build customer traffic and to cross-sell additional offers of complimentary goods and services.

Customer assistance plays a key role in customer satisfaction. It is the remaining merchandising area that is lacking or underdeveloped in many direct marketing offers.

Promotional Incentives

Sales incentives are inducements that offer extra value to the buyer and are often used to generate an immediate response. Coupons, samples, premiums, contests, sweepstakes, specialty advertising, and tie-in offers are the most commonly employed means. Direct marketers distribute coupons in newspapers, magazines, and mail; via the Internet; by fax; on and in packages; and through door-to-door delivery and advertising supplements. You can expect to increase your conversion rate every time you include some form of coupon with the offer. Coupons are one of the most important tactics you can use to nudge customers toward a favorable response. Sometimes a free sample will get the prospect involved through hands-on experience.

A premium is merchandise given to the buyer free of charge or at a substantial price reduction as an inducement. It's essentially a bonus given to a buyer or prospect. A self-liquidating premium requires the buyer to pay something for the premium; direct premiums are free gifts given at the time of purchase; mail-in premiums require a proof of purchase; and continuity premiums require buyers to make repeat purchases. What you are trying to do when you include a premium with the offer is to reward the customer for making the right decision. Purchase an item for $29 and receive a reward valued at $10.

Contests require that participants compete for rewards, such as solving a puzzle. Typically, contests require an entry fee or a purchase in order to participate. Buyers win in a sweepstakes only by chance. Examples of sweepstakes are matching (winning number must match a preselected number), instant win (winning number is revealed by rubbing off a covering), and program learning (winning entry is selected from a group of entries that have the correct information provided by sponsor's label, mail package, or ad). According to the psychology of sweeps, you can expect higher conversion rates (prospects to customers) because respondents feel obligated to buy even though no purchase is necessary. In using sweepstakes, you are banking on the belief by participants that a purchase will increase their odds of winning.

Specialty advertising is merchandise imprinted with the firm's name, logo, and perhaps ad and are given without obligation. The products should be useful and appropriate for the targeted buyer. Beer cozies given to children, for example, would not be well received.

Risk Reducers

There is always risk in decision making. Customers face financial risk, social risk, functional risk, and other risks associated with buying, using, and processing a product. You should do everything you can to reduce or eliminate as much of the risk as possible. Offers that include warrantees, guarantees, returns, product trials, and maintenance contracts substantially reduce the risks of buying.

Terms and Conditions

Make sure that buyers understand the financial plan for paying for the product. Credit in the form of "charge it!" "buy now, pay later," "easy terms available," and "sixty days same as cash" are all notices showing that credit is a basic ingredient. Credit may be a compelling component of the offer. Accepting credit cards is also a credit option. Buyers expect to pay the way that is most secure and convenient for them.

If you offer free shipping and handling, be sure that the customer doesn't have to do the math. The customer would appreciate the value of the offer without the extra work. Free shipping an initial offer over a certain size is something you should give careful consideration to before finalizing the offer, because shipping costs could be expensive.

All offers should have a built-in time constraint. A sense of urgency is an important element in the decision-making process. Offers should clearly state and reinforce the fact that the offer is special and will not last. One time-based tactic is a "snapper/penalty" clause. The "snapper" is a time limit—for example, 50 percent discount for the next 72 hours—while the "penalty" is the loss of the discount if the buyer fails to respond within the stated time period. Setting quantity limits suggests that the product is special and in high demand. Perceived value can be added by offering multiple units or greater quantities at discounted prices. "Buy one, get one free!" is a value enhancer.

The continuity offer helps establish a closer relationship with the customer. A subscription involves a fixed number of units for an established price, such as magazines, collectables, books, and collections. Automatic shipping plans involve the buyer authorizing products over a period of time. The key to these plans is that the buyer must say "no" to not buying the product.

STEP 4: STRUCTURE THE OFFER

Not only important is what you say important, but how you say it is equally important. The right message is the key element here. You can use either a logical or an emotional approach, or perhaps a combination of the two.

Using a logical approach, you present factual information about the offering and then show the buyer why the acceptance of the offer is the right choice. It relies on rational, practical, functional, and economical justification for accepting the offer.

The emotional appeal speaks not to what the buyer thinks, but to what they feel (pride, fear, love) and believe (free speech, nationalism, right to dissent), and to their loyalty (buy American), security (we sell only brand-name merchandise), tradition and security (serving you for 20 years), and belonging (where personal values are valued).

Whether logical or emotional, the successful offer should be simple, unique, exciting, exclusive, believable, significant, and valued.

Our next concern is the means by which the right message is communicated. What distinguishes one direct-marketing format from another is the type of communication media used by the seller and the type of mechanism available to the consumer. You can typically use direct selling, direct mail, mail order, and electronic marketing.

Direct selling is direct-to-consumer marketing through personal explanation and demonstration of products. This can be accomplished face-to-face or over the phone. Telemarketing operations are either inbound or outbound. Inbound practices involve motivating the prospect to call a toll-free number to take advantage of the seller's offer. Outbound telemarketing involves the seller calling qualified prospects (individuals that fit the customer profile and who do not appear on the "do not call" list) in order to create awareness, gain trial, commitment, and postsell (ensure their satisfaction). The third form is multilevel, in which the pyramidal nature is geared toward recruiting new distributors in order to sell a variety of goods and services.

Direct mail uses the postal service to communicate the offer, usually a mail package, catalog, or videolog. The outer envelope, letter, brochure, and order form must be used creatively. Catalogs present goods and services by means of photos, descriptions, sketches, and other visual tools. Videologs are videotapes using both sight and sound stimuli.

Mail order operations use print and broadcast. Customers are asked to respond by mail, telephone, or via a Web site. Home shopping combines two of America's favorite pastimes—watching television and going shopping. QVC (Quality, Value, and Convenience) Network and the Home Shopping Channel are two of the biggest home-shopping venues. The infomercial is another type of mail order operation—typically a 30-minute ad that mixes information and entertainment with a sales presentation.

Electronic shopping is a direct response communication channel in which the seller interacts with prospects and buyers via interactive television or personal computer. This form brings together four key patronage factors—convenience, selection, customization, and efficiency.

STEP 5: TEST THE OFFER

The final offer should be one that has been tested on a limited basis with a representative sample of your target market. The complexity of the previous steps creates a need for testing the offer before going to market. Given all of the alternatives, what combination would be the most effective? The best answer to that question is to ask prospective buyers and responders.

SUMMARY

Following is a summary of key points to consider when developing and implementing the right offer:

- Value offers or propositions are created using a five-step process— conceptualizing, targeting, creating, structuring, and testing the offer.

- An offer is a contract, deal, or proposition between the seller and prospect that is designed to secure a favorable transaction and relationship among all parties.

- Good offers are important, distinctive, affordable, superior, hard to duplicate, beneficial, compelling, tangible, and profitable.

- Value equations are implicit promises made by the direct marketer to the prospect that they will deliver a particular package of values sought by the prospect.

- Value is a function of some combination of product design, product quality, product mix, product benefits, pricing points, supporting services, promotional incentives, risk reducers, terms, and conditions.

- Every offer must make the right appeal in terms of the right message to the right audience through the right media.

Chapter 9

CREATIVE MARKETING COMMUNICATIONS: CREATING AND DELIVERING THE RIGHT MESSAGE

William J. Hauser

The medium is the message.

—Marshall McLuhan

Someone once said, "A picture is worth a thousand words." But in today's highly competitive, multichannel marketing environment, one really needs to ask whether that picture (i.e., piece of creative) is really worth a $1,000. Creative marketing communications require the skill of blending the science of marketing with the art of communicating. To be successful one cannot just create pretty pictures, one must use those pictures to generate profitable direct marketing campaigns. The best creative marketing campaigns require the marketer to do a significant amount of homework before even conceptualizing the work.

Developing and sending the right message to the right consumer at the right time is the heart of any successful direct marketing creative. Like a work of art, the piece must immediately shine through the clutter, grab the viewer's attention, and, most important, speak directly to him or her. Glitzy collateral pieces and elaborate Web sites are just pictures at an exhibition. If the viewers do not understand or relate to them, they will not buy. Individuals want to be "wowed." This wow-factor is as much understanding the individual and getting the right message to him or her as it is creating the message itself. Direct marketers need to know their customers to truly delight them.

WHAT IS CREATIVE?

The term "creative" has two separate, but very related, meanings. One is a set of ideas, while the other is the product of those ideas. In the first case, being creative requires the knack of understanding the right message and then framing it in such a way that it uniquely cuts through the clutter, attracts the viewers' attention, gains and maintains their interest, and, most important, calls them to action. In this sense, being creative is an attitude or state of mind. It is not just thinking outside the box, it is creating a new and unique box that not only entices customers, but also keeps them interested and wanting to return for more information. In electronic marketing this is known as "stickiness." By stickiness we mean to, first of all, provide the honey to attract the customer's attention and, once caught up in the attraction, whet their appetite (i.e., motivate) to return for more and more of its unique flavor.

The other type of creative is the actual product of one's imagination. It is the pictures, the sounds, and the words that not only entertain but also inform. This creative can be in the form of a four-color print advertisement, an infomercial, a piece of direct mail, a billboard, or even a Web site. It can be an elaborate and highly sophisticated piece of technology at one end of the continuum or a simple word or phrase at the other end. For example, the simplicity of the Nike "swoosh" has generated more brand recognition than the majority of sophisticated campaigns that have appeared in the last decade. Take a check mark, change it ever so slightly, call it a swoosh, and, low and behold, you have not only created a very successful campaign and logo, you have created a cultural icon. Its genius is in its simplicity.

THE DAWNING OF CREATIVE

Once upon a time a cavewoman was gnawing away at a piece of raw deer meat when lightning struck a nearby tree. Startled, the cavewoman jumped up and ran away from the burning tree. As she hurried away, the piece of meat fell from her hands into the fire. After finally regaining her composure, our hero remembered how hungry she had been, how good the deer meat would have tasted, and how hard it would be to find another meal. Motivated by pangs of hunger, she decided that it was worth the risk of injury to go back to the burning tree and retrieve the day's entree. Our cavewoman carefully moved closer to the fire and cautiously grabbed the now sizzling piece of meat from it. In the process, she saved the meat but burned her hand. Her attention quickly changed from the overdue meal to the painful hand. She carefully set the meat aside and sought some cooling mud to relieve her pain. Once accomplished, a small voice inside of her reminded her of the hunger she had long postponed. She returned to the spot where she had left the now cooling deer meat and began her long overdue repast.

As she began to eat, our cavewoman contemplated the events of the day. At the same time, her senses told her that there was something radically different about her meal. The meat looked different and it smelled different. She was afraid to actually taste it for fear that something was wrong. Her hunger, however, convinced her that she should try it anyway. After much trepidation, the cavewoman took the first bite. It tasted different but good. The concept of "hot" meals had just been invented (along with charcoal grilling, carcinogens, and the anti-red meat movement).

Our cavewoman was excited by her new discovery. She decided to share this treat with the other members of her clan. However, she knew she had to be very careful to protect the process of how to prepare the feast. After all, controlling this unique piece of information would increase her social standing within the clan. She knew that she had come across something unique; something that would make her special. Somehow, the cavewoman knew she had something that others would want, but how could she profit from it? She knew she had to tell others and, thus, the first creative marketing communication campaign was born.

THE FIRST CREATIVE CAMPAIGN

One can imagine, in a "Flintstone-esque" kind of way, an entrepreneurial tribe member, possibly our cavewoman herself, deciding on the best ways to share the cooked deer meat message. Using the limited technology available, our creative director decides that pictures may be the best. Finding the most traveled and best lit cave, she paints a picture of a caveperson sitting by a fire eating meat with what looks like smoke coming from the meat. Our creative director figures this is just enough information for others to become interested and ask for more information around the village. Thus, the art created a local buzz.

Our director decides that a promotional event is the next step. A tribal meeting is occurring in a couple of days. Why not introduce the entire village to the product then? Having already created the buzz, our director decides that maybe some direct interactive marketing is appropriate. She prepares a portion of cooked deer meat and then slowly walks between each of the hovels, letting the aroma spread and peaking the other tribe member's curiosity. Being a smooth operator, our director quickly leaves the scene but tells everyone she'll see them at the meeting.

Figuring that most of the tribe will be a little apprehensive to try the meat, she decides that a celebrity endorser may be the best approach. Because the shaman is not sure whether the gods approve this activity, she decides to go to the top warrior in the tribe. Playing on his ego, she finally persuades him to try the cooked deer meat. After trying the meat, three helpings worth, he decides he likes it and will help her. At the upcoming meeting he will be the first to try it and then motivate others to do so. But his endorsement comes at a cost. Our creative director will have to prepare him the cooked deer meat nightly for one cycle of the moon.

Just before the meeting, our director remembers that some of the villagers may not have had the opportunity to see the painting or smell the cooked meat. She decides that the reigning state-of-the-art communication media, drums, is the next tool in her plan. She persuades the local drummers to "tease" the audience with a message about something special that will happen at the meeting. Knowing that time is limited, she decides to send the message twice a day leading up to the meeting and then three times on the day of the event (frequency). Trying to maximize the number of people who will hear the drums (reach), she decides to have the message sent during the late morning and evening meals.

Now, considering our Flintstone-esque view of the world of the cave dweller, let's get even more far fetched. Our creative director contacts the local cave news station and invites them to the meeting to do a "live shot" of the latest find in food preparation. The reporter, dressed in his finest deerskin attire, explains to the television audience how the cavewoman was about to share her new find with her friends. As the cavewoman passes around the cooked meat and her friends begin to eat, the camera records looks of trepidation, curiosity, and then satisfaction. Our reporter comments that when people are through watching this telecast, they will most assuredly run out and try cooked meat. He ends his broadcast by saying that "cooked meat" will quickly become the hottest trend in cave households around the world.

It is important to look closer at our reporter. He also plays the role of marketer in this episode. As the well-respected, Stone E. Brook of CNN (Cave News Network), our reporter has built a substantial amount of credibility with his audience. Thus, when Stone speaks, audiences listen and believe what he says. If Stone says that cooked meat will be the hottest trend, then he must be right. As a member of his audience, I will want to be "in," so I will try to be the first in my village to follow the trend. Thus, in essence, I become the direct marketer for my village.

The introduction of the cooked deer meat was a huge success at the meeting. So much so that demand quickly outgrew supply. Our director had created a successful advertising campaign and decided to set up shop. Specializing in food preparation but running out of deer meat, she decided to see whether other meat (cows, sheep, dogs, etc.) may taste just as good. Not trusting her own tastes, our director brought eight of her friends together, offered them different types of cooked meat, and then asked their opinions. With this, the first focus group was completed and, since then, marketing has never been the same.

TWENTY-FIRST CENTURY CREATIVE IS MULTIDIMENSIONAL

While our cave creative director was pretty much limited to cave walls to draw the creative pictures, drums to communicate across short distances, and word of mouth to spread her message, creative messaging in the twenty-first century is truly multidimensional. Today's creative can be written or spoken. It can be one picture or an unlimited supply of electronic images. It can be delivered in so many different ways that our cave creative director's head would spin. However, no matter how complex and technologically advanced today's creative has become, its foundation still centers around three basic pillars: audience, message, and channel.

Direct marketing, as its name implies, is customer-centric relationship marketing that focuses on the individual or group of similar individuals. In reality, you are really marketing yourself to a group of one. But it takes many groups of one to make the campaign feasible and, especially, profitable. The trick long practiced by the best creative directors is to make the group feel that the message is specifically directed to each one of them individually. A recent excellent example of this is the U.S. Army's recruiting campaign centered on an "Army of One" creative message, developed by Leo Burnett Worldwide.

Traditional campaigns have focused on the target individual being part of a team with the skills and benefits coming from being a part of this team. The target individual is usually a young adult male or female that has recently graduated from high school and is trying to decide on the next path to take. Many factors influence their decision to join, including patriotism, commitment, learning applicable skills, and enhancing their self-esteem. The "Army of One" campaign successfully addressed these factors by suggesting that, by being part of the team, the individual will be provided with an environment in which he or she can continue to grow as a more complete person. That is, they will become an army of one.

At the heart of the best creative messages is a very simple goal: make the recipient feel comfortable. What is comfortable? From the recipient's perspective, being comfortable has many components. One major component of comfort is feeling secure and nonthreatened. Fast-paced, in-your-face messages may be exciting to some, but they can be intimidating to others. Likewise, asking someone to provide personal information or even purchase a product when they are not totally sure of why they are doing it can be very discomforting.

Comfort is also found in the recipient's perception that the message is one of the tools that a company is using to develop a good relationship with him or her. If recipients perceive that the sender knows them and understands their needs, likes, and dislikes, and then applies this information in the messages sent, it creates a feeling that the sender really does care. In turn, recipients feel that they can maintain and even enhance their relationship with that company.

Comfort is also based on consistency. It exists when you treat the recipient the way he or she wants to be treated each and every time you contact them. Inconsistency is confusing, intimidating, and may even increase the level of discomfort to the point at which the recipient feels the most comfortable by terminating the relationship.

Using a multichannel approach is another related way to increase the level of comfort. This is accomplished by sending the message through as many touch points or channels with which the recipient is comfortable. Remember, the recipient's preference of channels is the key driver. Arbitrarily flooding the recipient with messages through every available channel is not only a waste of the recipient's time and yours, it is also a waste of money. Different individuals feel more comfortable communicating through some channels rather than others. For example, a Generation Y individual may feel very comfortable receiving text messages or e-mails, but never reads a newspaper or magazine. On the other hand, seniors may feel most comfortable receiving mail or reading the message in a print advertisement. Not only is this less intimidating to this older audience, it allows them to control their environment and, therefore, maintain their level of comfort.

Twenty-first century creatives have more tools and channels available to them than at any point in history. They can use this array of tools to send their messages anywhere in the world at any time they please. Technology has provided today's direct marketer with the keys to cyberspace. But without a map or plan, way too many of these campaigns have ended up in a cyber-maze where all of the time, energy, and, especially, money are spent just trying to find the right direction in which to profitably move forward.

Marketing communications truly become creative when the appropriate messages are transmitted through the most appropriate channels that are linked together for maximum efficiency. This is integrated marketing at its finest and not just a bunch of loosely related words and pictures.

NOT JUST PICTURES

In reality, however, things have not changed that dramatically over the past few years (or thousands of years). Direct marketing creative is the tool that first attracts the individual's attention. Most creative types hope that some day their work will receive the rewards so richly deserved. But fantastic graphics and outstanding copy mean much more to a marketer than just pretty pictures. They are the message we are sending to the customer. Sounds pretty simple, but is it? What do the pictures really mean to the audience? Did they attract their attention, peak their interest, and motivate them to action? Did they understand the message and how long did it take them to "get it"? Creative must be from the audience's perspective or it is nothing more than pretty pictures.

The movie *Field of Dreams* gave us a famous line still used today: "If you build it, they will come." In our complex customer-centric environment, doing this may be much harder than you think. Who is "they"? Is "they" every person in the world, the majority of which will never see or even become aware of the product? Or is "they" a smaller targeted group of people who might be interested in and motivated to buy your product? The macroscopic "they" may provide you with billions of impressions with little or no return. The microscopic "they" may have a much smaller reach, but a reach that stands a much better probability of achieving positive results. For this reason, good creative is data driven. One cannot understand the audience's perspective if you don't know what it is. Understanding (even if only at a minimal level) your customers' needs, preferences, and lifestyles helps to create a picture that is "spot on" and, more important, provides the customer with the sense you know and are concerned about them.

Creative, nor the data gathering used to develop it, does not have to be expensive. There is a wealth of data readily available on most customers and, in many cases, it already rests in your files. What does your audience look like demographically, how do they think, and what is their past purchase behavior? By collecting and maintaining this information, you are better able to understand your audience and their expectations. At the same time, by using this information, you are able to gauge whether this is where you want to be or whether you need to design strategies to go after other audiences or segments.

One of the best marketing campaigns in recent years has been by a young, upstart magazine called *Mental_Floss*. The magazine was founded four years ago by two college students and is one of the fastest growing magazines in the country. Because the magazine had little or no money for advertising, they decided to use guerilla direct marketing tactics to spread the word about the magazine. First, as the magazine gained in popularity, word spread and magazines were passed from reader to reader and, in many cases, intentionally left in airports, businesses, doctor's offices, and other areas. The business manager for the magazine then used every available (and free) public relations tool available to get the magazine in front of the media. He wrote newspapers and radio stations, sending copies and suggesting that they have regular *Mental_Floss* articles in the newspapers and *Mental_Floss* moments on the radio shows. The uniqueness and quirkiness of the magazine caught on to the point that CNN Headline News runs a weekly *Mental_Floss* segment, radio stations regularly interview the magazine on topics of interest, and, because of copies passed on to a television producer and the spouse of a cast member, the magazine was prominently displayed on a number of "Friends" sitcom episodes. Within four years, the management at *Mental_Floss* has grown the enterprise to more than 100,000 subscribers to the magazine, three best-selling books, a board game, and thoughts of creating their own game show—all of this on a shoestring budget. It can be done!

CREATING THE MASTERPIECE

Did you ever view a piece of art and ask, "everyone says this is a masterpiece, but I don't get it"? Do you spend hours studying the picture or do you just move on? This also holds true for customers looking at print advertisements, Web sites, and other creative endeavors. The window of attention and understanding is extremely narrow. We teach students that if the viewer does not get the message in the first 15 seconds, they will probably move on. Ideally, the piece should become "sticky," that is, the viewer/reader should spend time observing it and then continue to return to it in the future. At the same time, the creative coupled with the message should leave the viewer excited, motivated, and wanting to do something (i.e., seek out additional information or purchase the product or service).

Step 1: Prepare the Canvas

Good creative is like painting a masterpiece. It requires knowledge, preparation, and execution. First, you must prepare your canvas. Who is your intended target audience? Why is this audience so important to you? Remember that while it would be great to include everyone in the world in your campaign, it is virtually impossible and cost-prohibitive to even attempt to do so. Today, the best creative directors take the time to understand their target audience before developing the creative piece. This does not need to be extremely time-consuming or expensive. Decide what information you already have available and what else you need to know. The data are probably right in front of you; it just needs to identified, organized, and, most important, adapted to your needs. Why not use this information to supplement and enhance your customer knowledge base?

Joel Sobelson, former chief creative director for Wunderman New York, one of the world's largest and best direct marketing advertising agencies, attributes much of his success to the fact that, with each project, he and his staff took the time to research their target audience before even conceptualizing the creative copy and artwork. They wanted to know what behaviors, attitudes, and opinions the audience had that would create "hot spots" or areas of interest the creative could build on. A large, traditionally adult-oriented vacation resort company came to Wunderman asking them to create a campaign that would change people's perceptions of the resort and entice families with children to begin using it. Sobelson researched both the current perceptions of the resort and what vacationing families (especially with small children) wanted in their vacation resort packages. Based on these findings, he and his staff were able to create a very successful, multichannel direct marketing campaign.[1]

A good first step is to create a profile of the target audience by identifying them demographically. What are their common characteristics? What do they look like? Are they young, old, or middle age? Are they predominantly male or female? What do they do for a living? Do they have families? How educated are they? At the macroscopic level, most of this information can be found online. Census data and generation-specific Web sites are just a click away. Can't think of where to start? Try typing some keywords or phrases into any of the available search engines and the process begins.

At the microscopic level, mine your customer databases for information. Most companies, no matter how small, have gathered a substantial amount of data on their customers. Customers provide this information thinking that it will help the company to better serve them. So why not collect it, organize it, and use it? Who are your existing customers? Do their demographic attributes reflect the audience to whom you are targeting your communications? If so, what pieces of knowledge does their information provide you? If not, where do you need to go to find this information? Market research is a viable, but usually expensive, option. Renting databases and lists is also acceptable, but it too can become expensive. More important, you still need to understand your audience to obtain the most useful lists.

As important as it is to understand your audience demographically, you also need to understand their lifestyles, interests, actions, and behaviors. Think of demographics as a tree's trunk and limbs, and lifestyles as its branches. We know who they are demographically (trunk), now we need to know how they live their lives (branches). Again, much of this information is readily available and accessible. Both online and traditional media consistently portray lifestyles and other trends. Your job is to shape these pieces of information into an accurate profile of your audience.

By doing this background work, you are deciding what textures you will use to paint your most meaningful picture. Likewise, by creating an actionable profile of your target audience, you are preparing your canvas for your creative masterpiece. However, a word of caution is offered here. All too often in the past, agencies and creative staffers have arbitrarily decided that they know what their target audience wants, needs, and likes. In many of the cases, however, these decision makers are not a part of the target audience, nor have they taken the time to look at life from the audience's perspective. By seeing your painting through your audience's eyes, you are giving your canvas the best possible texture.

Step 2: Select the Right Materials

Now that your canvas is ready, it's time to select the right materials, that is, what should the piece look like? Today's cyber-rich environment makes it easy to use digital sights and sounds only dreamed about a decade or two ago. Think of a Web site that you feel has great graphics, colors, music, streaming videos, and so on. Now quickly ask yourself what the Web site was about and, more important, what was the message it was trying to convey? If you can't answer these questions in 15 seconds or less, all that you have is a pretty picture with little or no perspective.

Knowing your audience will help you decide what your creative should look like. Remember, not everyone appreciates a Picasso. Decide which medium or media is the most appropriate to maximize the message. Ask yourself a bunch of questions about your audience. Do they regularly read newspapers and magazines? Do they like getting mail? Many people do. Do you remember as a child waiting to see whether the postman had any mail for you and how excited you became when you got some? Old habits stick with you. Also, you probably have never looked at it in this manner but most catalogs are keepsakes. While people may not keep them as fine pieces of art, they do keep them as references and put them in their magazine racks to refer to as needed. Keep in mind that printed material allows the recipients to take their time to view it, digest it, and then act on it. In its own way, this is stickiness.

Radio and television are extremely popular and reach millions of viewers. Television's primary purpose is creating the buzz. It attracts the viewers' attention and makes them aware. In a sense, it plants the seed. But this seed usually needs more to help it grow. A 15- or 30-second commercial can only say so much and is extremely expensive. This is another reason why knowing your audience is so important. Effective television advertising requires finding the best time, channel, and event or topic to maximize your reach. A favorable return on your television advertising dollar is really contingent on knowing when your audience is watching and what they are watching.

On the other hand, radio is all about frequency (no pun intended). Most individuals are usually doing something else while listening to the radio, so they need to quickly internalize the message. Because the message may not have their undivided attention, it needs to be repeated over and over. Thus, while the listener may not focus on the message each and every time he or she hears it, with constant repetitions the message gradually sinks in. In fact, think of the jingles on the radio and how quickly you start humming or singing them and wonder why you continue to do so. Mission accomplished.

But even television and radio may seem to be old school in today's technological environment. The Internet, with its multiple channels of communication, has opened a new 24/7 dialogue with audiences never seen before. You can now contact your customer through Web sites, blogs, podcasts, and, especially, e-mails. Web sites are great at presenting vast amounts of information in graphically entertaining ways. But if the Web site doesn't immediately define itself and quickly provide its offer, it is nothing more than one of a million pieces of cyber-clutter. The next time you look up something on a search engine ask yourself whether you actually found what you were looking for and then look at the thousands of sites you may need to click through before you find what you want.

Blogs and podcasts have become popular ways to target the message to the right audience, especially in the business-to-business environment. However, usually some other form of direct marketing is needed to initially drive someone to the message. For this reason, these tools appear to work better by helping to reinforce the customer relationship after it has been developed.

However, e-mail marketing may have the greatest potential of all these tools. Effective e-mail marketing requires a number of factors to make it successful. First, it must be targeted toward someone who is interested and wants to receive the message. Second, it is permission based (i.e., the recipient agrees to keep on receiving the e-mails). Third, it is personalized. Not only are the recipients interested in the e-mail to the point of wanting to continue communications, they feel comfortable enough to give you their permission to continue to do so. This is at the heart of creating strong ties with the customer and the foundation for customer relationship management.

One last tool is moving quickly on to direct marketing's radar screen. Today's world is a world of the cellular phone. Not only are cellular or mobile phones universally accepted, they have become the primary means of communication and messaging for millions of individuals. It really does make direct marketing a 1:1 endeavor. Recent changes in regulations and the continued competitive growth in telecommunications make it quite feasible to market directly to customers via their cell phones. Integrate this with global positioning satellite (GPS) capabilities and you will be able to direct your message to an individual anywhere in the world at any time you wish.

But, two huge stumbling blocks exist before this can successfully occur. First are the obvious issues of annoyance and privacy. Customers do not want their phones inundated with advertising, especially if they are paying for it. Also, being tracked down at anytime or any place not only leads to high levels of discomfort, but also increases the risk of invading one's privacy and subjecting their personal information to fraud and theft.

The second issue is more technical in nature. Not all communications on the phone will be voice messages. In fact, most may be text messages and graphics. But the current monitor or viewing screen is miniscule. How will you get everything on it in a way that is quick to read and digest? This canvas will need to be dramatically changed as will how the picture is portrayed. Will the message be graphics only, text only, or a combination of graphics, text, and voice over? Figure this out and you will become a megastar in direct marketing.

Step 3: Paint the Picture

Now that you have prepared the canvas and selected your paints, it's time to put brush to canvas. That is, implement the campaign. Like every good painting, the campaign needs perspective, which is best done by preparing an integrated communications plan. Depth of perspective comes by implementing a campaign that reaches as many touch points as the customer is comfortable with. The trick is organizing and integrating the media to maximize the effect. First, television, radio, and telemarketing can be used strategically to create awareness and interest. The second step is to then provide the customers with information to help them better understand the message and to become more attached (stickiness) to it. Direct response mail, print advertising, and Web sites are used here to provide the recipient with the information needed in the manner that he or she feels most comfortable digesting it. The third step is to secure the relationship through direct contact with the individual. Both telemarketing and, especially, permission-based e-mails can be very effective here.

Depending on your audience, the above techniques can be used in any number of combinations. The focus, however, must be on planning and implementing the right combinations at the right time in the right sequence. These are the brush strokes that give your communications their unique feel. Remember, sometimes, the minimum number of strokes may be the best. For years Little Tikes, the children's toy company, grew its customer base with little or no mass advertising. Instead, they used two very strong and cost-efficient direct marketing techniques to paint their picture. First, each package containing the purchased toy had a small catalog of related Little Tikes products in it. The customer, having purchased at least one Tikes toy and knowing their reputation for quality, could browse through the catalog and then identify other products they wanted to purchase. They could then take the catalog with them to their favorite retailer to purchase or order the product or they could order directly by phone or from Little Tike's Web site. Second, and even more important, Little Tike's products had almost a cult following among parents and grandparents. Much of Little Tike's advertising was successfully accomplished through word-of-mouth advertising as generations of families and their acquaintances passed on Little Tike's toys and then continued to spread the positive brand buzz to others. The irony of this excellent form of direct marketing is that Little Tike's products are so durable and long lasting that when families outgrow them they are passed on to others. In a sense, the passing on of the products and their resale through yard sales and the like became one of the biggest hurdles for the company to overcome.

Finally, as the recipient of your work of art, the consumers' attention is gained and their interest peaks. They take the time to study it closely and even imagine themselves in the picture. Most important, they feel comfortable that the picture is speaking directly to them and thus they develop a close connection to it. You have created a masterpiece and they are willing to purchase your product.

SUMMARY

Twenty-first-century direct marketing has come a long way since the first creative director. The marketer's toolkit is loaded with a wide variety of tools and technologies. We can communicate our messages in any number of shapes and forms and touch our customers at any time in just about any place. But, in reality, the creative process has changed little since the early days of wall drawings and drums. Successful creative is much more than pretty pictures. It is getting the right message to the right customer at a time and in a way that the individual wants to receive it.

The best customers are comfortable customers. They are comfortable with you, your message, and how that message is delivered. An excellent way to make customers comfortable is to know and understand them. Take the time to gather data on your customers and then use this information to develop and target creative messages that will make each individual feel that the message is especially for him or her.

Remember, good creative is like painting a masterpiece. The work attracts attention, heightens interest, and draws the viewer back to it again and again. With few exceptions, a masterpiece is the end product of the painter's blood, sweat, and tears. Before you paint the final picture make sure your canvas is well prepared.

Learn all you can about your target audience: Who are they, what do they look like, and how do they think and act? Once this is done, select the right materials. What should the creative look like and what is the best way (or ways) to deliver it to your audience? This is done by objectively viewing it through the recipient's eyes. With this being accomplished, you can now paint your masterpiece. Make sure to give it perspective by developing and implementing an integrated communications plan. Strategically maximize your message's effectiveness by using the most appropriate direct marketing techniques in a sequence that attracts, informs, and motivates.

You have now created and delivered the right message to your most profitable audience. Let the campaign do its magic and then take the time to reflect on the work done. Finally, take a minute to think about our cavewoman creative director and the first creative campaign. Getting hungry? How about a nice venison steak?

Chapter 10

DIRECT MARKETING CHANNELS: SELECTING AND EMPLOYING THE RIGHT MEDIA

Bruce D. Keillor

> The best product in the world is worthless if you can't get it to your customer.
>
> —Henry Ford

As we have seen in the previous chapters, the whole notion of direct marketing goes well beyond the image of "bothersome" marketing that exists in the minds of many people, business, and customers alike. Just as the old-school approach of communicating to masses of potential customers through, say, television, or radio ads is no longer universally effective, neither is the stereotype of direct marketing being the annoying phone call at dinner time. Truly effective marketing must have the targeted, creative, customized qualities that define direct marketing in the twenty-first century. This brings us to the problem of actually employing direct marketing activities to successfully gain access to customers. In this chapter, we will explore how direct marketing has changed the concept of marketing "channels," or the means through which the firm gains access to customers, and how winning companies can begin to create a first-class direct marketing channel strategy.

In the past, any discussion of marketing channels was all about how a firm could construct a distribution network that would bridge the gap between the product's location and the customer. The focus was on physical distribution and logistics that, by their very nature, create both a tangible and intangible breech between the firm and its customers making relationship management exceedingly difficult. This meant dealing with wholesalers, retailers, physical distribution, inventory control, and all the hundreds, perhaps thousands, of related logistical challenges that go along with "moving product." In the new world of direct marketing, some of these variables (like wholesalers) can drop out of the equation, others (like retailing) take on a new look, while still others (like inventory control) have to be adapted. The result is a direct channel structure that, when properly employed, not only places control firmly in the hands of the originating firm, but also is available to firms of all types and sizes.

Consider for a moment the retail book industry. The traditional channel model, still used to some extent by major chains such as Barnes and Noble, is incredibly resource-heavy when it comes to physical distribution and inventory control. Potential customers have to take the time to actually go to the store—and the only way to entice them to do this is to provide an inventory containing a wide (and costly) range of books and related products. To offset the high costs of traditional retailing, these companies offer high-margin products such as coffee and pastry. Contrast that with the direct marketing approach used by Amazon.com, where it is possible not only to access and purchase the same types of product but also to have other related products promoted seamlessly as the customer moves through the purchase process. Not only does this direct marketing approach applied by Amazon. com alter the business-consumer marketing of books, it changes the business-to-business book market to the benefit of small and medium-size companies. Where many specialty book shops were geographically bounded and highly dependent on word-of-mouth promotion and repeat customers, sometimes to the point of a monthly, hand-to-mouth existence, working through Amazon.com exponentially increases their market coverage *and* dramatically expands Amazon.com's product line—the ever-elusive win-win situation.

In an industry in which not long ago conventional wisdom said a customer had to be able to physically handle a book before purchase, direct marketing principles are forcing established players, like Barnes and Noble, to reconfigure their marketing channel strategy, thereby changing the way they approach accessing customers. The combination of being able to easily electronically "browse" a much wider selection of books and the availability of products previously determined to be "hard to get" is a powerful competitive advantage.

CONSTRUCTING A DIRECT MARKETING CHANNEL: TOOLS OF THE TRADE

Clearly, if a channel is to be truly "direct," using the old pieces that formed the basis of a traditional marketing channel is not an option. In a world in which wholesalers, distributors, retailers, and so on serve as filters and interact in a way that is dominated by a jockeying for power and controlling dependencies (i.e., Wal-Mart), access to the customer is anything but direct. The fundamental premise behind constructing a *direct* marketing channel is to remove all those filters and barriers and construct a channel to customers that is directly controlled by the individual firm. In short, our direct marketing channel cuts out the middleman—to the benefit of the firm and its customers. In a direct marketing channel strategy, the single, definitive word is *relationship*.

When it comes to building a direct marketing channel there are four major tools: (1) telemarketing, (2) direct mail, (3) e-mail, and (4) Internet Web sites. If properly used, each has its own unique advantages. Each tool also has a stereotyped image in the minds of many, which could make it unsuitable for any firm that valued its image in the marketplace. Remember what we have established in previous chapters. Those stereotypes of direct marketing are no more reflective of *true* direct marketing than the old movies *Used Cars* or *Tin Men* are of professional selling. When a firm uses these direct marketing tools in a way that plays to each tool's individual strengths, not only can the firm construct a highly effective channel to its customers, but also the stereotypes quickly fall by the wayside. There is a caveat: These four types of direct marketing channels are reflective of those most widely and generally applied.

The discussion in this chapter is not necessarily all-inclusive or exhaustive. For example, as product offerings become more specialized or less frequently purchased, other direct channels, such as online auctions, may become viable. The channel options can be practically and effectively applied by all firms, large or small, while other direct channels, which could be very effective under specific circumstances, may not be generally applicable to all firms at all times.

Telemarketing

Of all the direct marketing tools available to any business, telemarketing may be the most maligned. The stereotype of an unwanted call during dinner time has virtually made "direct" marketing synonymous with "bothersome" marketing and those engaged in telemarketing have often done little to dispel this image. We have all been on the receiving end of this type of approach and probably all found it equally annoying. When our children were younger, we simply handed the phone over to them. A three-year-old child can be a remarkable conversationalist, but not necessarily an effective target market. At the same time, it is probably a safe bet to say we have all responded to a telemarketing contact in a positive way and, perhaps, even found the contact helpful. We just have a tendency to remember negative experiences.

In considering a direct marketing strategy and the tactical tools available to any firm, it is important to move beyond simple stereotypes and consider each tool's unique capability. This is especially true with telemarketing. Consider this: If your firm was offered a channel through which you could access customers quickly, cheaply, and in large numbers, it would seem to be a pretty good foundation for establishing a profitable link with your customer base. Add to this the ability to segment and target your contacts as well as interact with them to clarify offers and answer any questions they might have. Sounds like a winning combination. That's what *good* telemarketing can do. But to achieve successful results, it is vital to, as Clint Eastwood's Dirty Harry says, "know [its] limitations."

A good telemarketer will tell you success lies, in large part, in the ability to empathize with your contact. Being able to "get inside" their minds is the first big step in effectively employing telemarketing to access customers. Start by considering the timing of the call or contact. Is it a time the customer would find convenient? Remember, dinnertime may be a great time of day to catch people at home but that doesn't mean they will be interested. Is the contact made at a time when they are receptive to the offer?

A good example of this principle in action would be any one of several of the larger mortgage and finance companies who have discovered the key to successful telemarketing revolves around these simple issues of timing and receptivity. By combining these two concepts, financial services firms have discovered an evening call to the customer's home during the first few days of each month produces the best success rate. Superior timing is achieved not only because the customer is more likely to be at home but also because the first few days of any month is when mortgage payments—generally the single largest monthly expenditure in any household—are most likely to be foremost in the customer's mind. The customer's receptivity feeds off of this timing issue and is supported by the fact that they are physically in the home, upon which the offer revolves, at the time of contact. Combine this with the targeting and positioning principles already discussed, and telemarketing can be a formidable weapon.

Telemarketing can also be effective in the business-to-business marketing arena. Technology Concepts, Inc., a small Minnesota-based software firm selling to local real estate associations around the country, uses telemarketing to set up their other direct marketing activities. By knowing when each association's software licensing contracts expire (often a matter of public record), the firm knows exactly who to call and when to maximize the customer's receptivity to purchasing a new software product.

Direct Mail

Like telemarketing, direct mail suffers from a well-established stereotype in the marketplace: It's junk mail. Just as the telemarketing call has historically been approached using the quantity-over-quality strategy, when it comes to customer contact so has direct mail been characterized as the pile of unsolicited "junk" many of us receives every day. In the United States, depending on the addressee's demographics, estimates of the number of direct mail pieces a person receives in a single day is as high as 10 per day. Obviously much of this is wasted on the receiver. Yet, by playing to its unique strengths, direct mail can be an excellent means to establish customer access.

While telemarketing's success hinges, to a large extent, on timing and receptivity, the success of a direct mail campaign is built on recipient targeting and effective information use. Stepping back from the characterization of direct mail as "junk," a closer look reveals its two fundamental strengths: (1) the ability to target, and (2) the ability to convey *lasting* information.

The information needed to initiate a direct mail campaign is readily available and as easy to obtain as the information required in telemarketing. With direct mail, however, there is an important quality difference when it comes to contact information. The telephone numbers used as a basis for customer access in a telemarketing campaign do not, in and of themselves, provide much information about the customer, which could improve the quality of the contact.

Put another way, in general, it is very difficult to effectively segment a market using phone numbers. The address of a customer, however, can provide a wealth of information, mostly demographic, which can be tremendously helpful in effectively segmenting a market and then reaching the selected target or targets. Addresses provide the ability to identify customers by income (using housing prices, taxes, etc.), specific geographic areas (using zip codes), likely competitors (using basic mapping technology), and a firm's ability to gain access to the customer or potential customer (using location data). Being able to quickly identify *quality* contacts cannot be over-emphasized when trying to construct a solid, long-term channel for customer access.

Building on this notion of improved quality customer contact is the potential lasting impact of the information communicated via direct mail. No matter how much interaction a good telemarketing contact is able to establish, it is, in the end, a fleeting intangible experience. Direct mail, on the other hand, not only has the ability to provide a large quantity of tangible, visible information, but also this tangibility provides a shelf life for the offer that otherwise would not have existed. Provided that a given direct mail piece is able to demonstrate interest, or relevance, to its recipient, then there is a high likelihood they will retain the offer, at least for some period of time, for later reference.

A good example of the utilization of these principles in the use of direct mail is a campaign by Summit Racing Equipment located just outside of Akron, Ohio. Knowing the importance of not only being able to target the direct marketing of their specialty products, but also the need to provide product information in a lasting format, the firm's direct mail catalog serves as both a promotional piece and a reference guide complete with technical assistance contacts. Similarly, Technology Concepts, Inc. (already mentioned in regard to effective business-to-business telemarketing) follows up their initial phone contacts with sample discs of the software, which can be shared within the targeted organization to build product familiarity and open a basis for communication between the firm and the potential customer organization.

E-mail

The image that e-mail must overcome is not much different from that of telemarketing: bothersome and annoying. While telemarketing is a proactive form of contact with a customer, initiated by a firm, e-mail is more passive in the sense that the recipient has much more control over what, if any, information is received. Regardless of the fact that we may have received unsolicited electronic contacts from a firm we have found useful, virtually everyone with an active e-mail address has been the target of a regular stream of "spam," e-mail that is indiscriminately sent out to huge number of recipients.

The lure of such an approach is obvious: It is quick, cheap, and available to just about any size organization. Yet the quality of such a "shotgun" approach in accessing customers is, like the mass television ad campaigns of years gone by, highly suspect. For example, a Midwest state university employed e-mail mailing lists to recruit students to its executive MBA program. More than 50,000 contacts were made worldwide yielding exactly one applicant. Not an overwhelming result.

So the question becomes how can the unique advantages (quick, cheap, mass contacts, etc.) be harnessed to achieve *quality* results. The key lies in applying e-mail as a channel to customers using concepts discussed in previous chapters, specifically, identifying and reaching the right target market with the right offer. The principles underlying these activities need not be revisited. Rather, in the context of establishing effective direct marketing channels, the important issue at hand is to create the link between the organization's customer strategy and selling proposition. In the case of e-mail, the basic foundation of such a link is twofold: credibility and relevance.

Few things can be more damaging to the credibility of an e-mail contact than to have the recipient's system flag the message as "spam." While it may or may not be within the control of an individual organization to get around network spam filters, it is possible to address the perceived credibility of the message. To that end, one of the fundamentally most important things a firm can do to achieve the level of credibility necessary for the recipient to read the message is to identify, not hide, the source as it appears on the sender's address line and to use the subject line to summarize the content of the message—much like the tagline in an advertisement. Increasingly, security-conscious consumers will not open electronic messages that do not come from a readily identified source and that do not have a specific message.

Coupled with the need for credibility is the need for relevance. Using the subject line on an electronic message provides the link between the two. As discussed in chapter 8, an effective selling proposition is key if an organization wants to move a potential customer to action. It is the responsibility of the components that make up the direct marketing channel, in the case of e-mail in particular, to establish relevance. Using a subject line that "grabs" the recipient's attention, coupled with the application of the targeting principles discussed in chapter 6, establishes the conduit for communicating the offer to the customer—exactly what a marketing channel is supposed to do.

Geerling & Wade, a wine merchant based in New England, is extremely effective in using e-mail to establish and maintain relationships both with individuals and corporate clients. They understand each group's buying cycle, clearly identify themselves in any electronic communications, and explicitly state the offer in the subject line—exactly like an old-fashioned advertising tagline.

Internet/Web Sites

The fourth, and final, generally accepted direct marketing channel is the Internet, or Web sites. In contrast to the three channels already discussed, the use of Web sites would appear on the surface to be a passive, rather than a proactive, channel outlet. However, there is more to the effective use of a Web site than simply constructing a home page and listing the site with the usual search engines. Although these activities are clearly a start, a truly successful channel strategy that incorporates Web sites utilizes the single characteristic that sets the site apart: its ability to establish and maintain an ongoing, direct relationship with the customer. Tracking site visits and usage is an accepted activity among all organizations, large and small, that employ Web sites. But this alone does not establish any ongoing relationship with its customer base. The site must incorporate the relationship-oriented components of ease of use and specialized information or links to other relevant sites to create a value-added experience for the customer/visitor.

Once the customer has located the site, the extent to which it is user-friendly is paramount. Although the term "user-friendly" can encompass myriad possibilities, a review of home pages commonly identified as model direct marketing sites reveals some commonalities: ease of navigation, accessible information, and the ability to complete a transaction. Building these into any Web site represents the first major step in creating an effective channel to the customer.

Netflix is an excellent example of such a site. Conventional wisdom, when it came to video rentals, said customers viewed such activity as essentially a short-term impulse purchase that required a large selection, which applied very well to the business model of Blockbuster Video. Through a combination of well-designed navigation, an organized presentation of a large selection of videos searchable using a variety of inputs, and ease of purchasing that differentiated Netflix from Blockbuster by delivering the videos directly to the customer, with no time limit and a prepaid return package, Netflix has used their direct marketing to overcome the economies of scale associated with a nationwide video operation and has become a serious threat to the established industry leader.

Taking relationship-building within the direct marketing context one step further, including information or active links to related sites provides a value-added component that can move the customer from simply satisfied to "delighted." Research shows that the firm that can go the extra mile and delight the customer has established a relationship in which the customer is more likely to return on an increasing basis, purchase more per visit, and create significant levels of positive word-of-mouth promotion. Such a site can vault what might have been a small, local specialty firm onto the national, or even international, stage.

Furthermore, firms that focus on traditional business-to-business wholesale business, such as TireRack, one of the largest tire distributors in the country, have been able to expand into direct-to-consumer sales, while increasing their business-to-business sales, by tailoring their Web sites. In the case of TireRack.com, it is possible for consumers to select the right tire application for their individual needs as well as for retailers to obtain tires for their own unique inventory needs.

MULTICHANNEL MARKETING STRATEGY: PUTTING THE PIECES TOGETHER

Having covered the basic cornerstones of direct marketing channels, we need to step back and consider a key point: It is not necessary (or even advisable) to build your channel using just one form of the four basic options. The firms, both large and small, that tend to be most frequently identified as successful direct marketers tend to use a multichannel approach. As the term multichannel implies, it is quite realistic to combine the different channel options. Alternatively, multiple applications of the same channel may be the answer. The trick is to identify the right combination.

One British university found that, when marketing management training programs to local governments, the right combination of direct mail and telemarketing seems to produce the best results. After trying several campaigns using an e-mail and Web site combination, they realized that, although on the surface the electronic approach looked relatively cheap and had a wide potential reach, the old adage "you get what you pay for" rang true for their particular set of circumstances. The intention was to lead with an e-mail that would form the basis of the offer and then use a link in the message to redirect the targeted recipient to the university's management training home page.

The problem encountered was twofold. First, in the finest tradition of governments at all levels the world over, the local councils (courtesy of Her Majesty's government) had all invested in a large amount of technology and software. Good news for an electronically based direct marketing campaign. Not. Just as owning a Ferrari doesn't mean a person can drive, having the technology didn't necessarily mean the folks in the local government offices knew how to use it, and in some cases, they knew just enough to be dangerous (throw the Ferrari keys to a 16-year-old boy). In implementing the software applications, many of the local officials adopted the "more-is-better" approach, in particular with the e-mail filters. This resulted in many e-mails outside the network not reaching the intended recipient and, in at least one case, no outside e-mails at all making it through the filters, including those from other local councils and government agencies. Others had the opposite problem: no filtering at all, resulting in overloaded mailboxes and crashed systems.

The second problem was that those messages that did get through didn't hit the true target market. While it is true that the recipients would be potential participants in a management training course, they did not make the decision whether or not they would actually participate. That decision was left to their superiors. In short, the message was being received (when it was received) by the potential *consumer* but not the actual *buyer*—an important distinction to make and a crucial connection to establish. In many ways the problem is the same as that faced by breakfast cereals—convincing a child to eat chocolate in the morning is easy, getting the parents to buy it is another matter.

The trick to success lay in using a multichannel approach to link the buyers and consumers through a combination of direct mail and telemarketing. First, local council supervisors were identified and mailed a letter, using university envelopes and letterhead, describing the program and directing them to the university's management training program. A few days later calls were made with the simple objective of identifying "hot," "warm," and "cold" leads. Those in the "hot" and "warm" categories were then mailed simple bifold brochure to be distributed within the office. Follow-up calls were made first as a courtesy to determine whether the brochures had been received (and if they had been distributed along with the level of interest). A final call was made to "close" the deal, which may have involved sending application materials, directing online registration, or in some cases scheduling an on-site office visit. While not as inexpensive as the electronic approach, in this particular case, the more personal and directed use of direct mail and telemarketing proved to be the multichannel answer.

The use of multiple channels is an example of expanding the *width* of the channel strategy. Another option is expanding the *depth* of the channel strategy. One common and effective approach is to use multiple forms of e-mail, such as an initial mass mailing to reach a large number of potential buyers and consumers with an offer and then, based on their responses, establish an ongoing and focused, yet arm's length, relationship. This approach is especially effective for impulse-type purchases, such as books, movies, and music; personal or sensitive products, such as pharmaceuticals; and cyclical or seasonal products, such as flowers, candy, greeting cards, and gift baskets. Although this example is just directed at e-mail, the principle could also be applied within any of the other channel options.

ACTIONS AND REACTIONS: DIRECT MARKETING CHANNELS' STRENGTHS AND WEAKNESSES

As your science teacher used to say, for every action there is an equal and opposite reaction. Although that may be a bit strong in evaluating the strengths and weaknesses of each channel option, it is important to recognize that each channel option has positive and negative characteristics.

Strengths

While for any given firm there may be specific advantages, the strengths listed in figure 10-1 are generally identified as universal for each individual direct marketing channel. Telemarketing has always been recognized as an inexpensive means of establishing direct contact with a potential customer. What is often overlooked is that telemarketing, when done properly, can be personal, interactive, and coordinated so that the timing of the contact matches the receiver's receptivity and, perhaps most important, has the ability to produce directly measurable results. Direct mail, on the other hand, while not allowing for personal interaction, has a distinctly different set of unique strengths. Typically more expensive than telemarketing, direct mail can be effectively targeted, is generally viewed as nonintrusive, and can provide a lasting impact because of its tangibility and visual, information-rich nature.

At the same time, the more recently emerged technology-based channels each combine some of the strengths of the more traditional telemarketing and direct mail channels with advantages only

Figure 10-1 Strengths of Direct Marketing Channels

Telemarketing	_Direct Mail_
• Personal • Interactive • Timed • Inexpensive • Measurable	• Targeted • Non-Intrusive • Lasting Impact • Visual • Information-Rich
Electronic Mail	_Internet/Web Sites_
• Mass Contacts • Inexpensive • Impersonal • Confidential • Recipient Controlled	• Interactive • User-Controlled • Information Source • Customizable • Data Generator

available through technology. Like direct mail, e-mail allows for mass contact. It is also relatively inexpensive, impersonal (senders and recipients can maintain a comfortable distance), discrete, confidential, and controlled by the recipient (they can read it, save it, or delete it). Like telemarketing, the results of an e-mail campaign can also be measured for success fairly accurately. The use of the Internet and Web sites has, like direct mail, the potential for conveying information over a long period of time. However, unlike direct mail, this information can be regularly updated, which, combined with the fact that it is user initiated, means this channel can quickly become a value-added product feature. Added to this is the bonus of the data and customer feedback that Internet sites can quickly and easily provide.

Weaknesses

As one might expect, especially given the stereotypes associated with direct marketing, we need to recognize the weaknesses or limitations of each channel option as well. We all know that telemarketing can be intrusive and has been overused, making it difficult to engage contacts. The advent of caller ID and the national "do not call" list further exacerbates these problems. Direct mail also has been overused—just consider the amount of "junk" mail you receive on any given day. Chances are that most, if not all, of these relatively expensive (production, postage, etc.) pieces go straight into the garbage. If they don't, the offer can easily become outdated, which leads to customer confusion and dissatisfaction.

Figure 10-2 Weaknesses of Direct Marketing Channels

Telemarketing	*Direct Mail*
• Intrusive	• Over-used
• Over-used	• Expensive
• Can be Screened	• Easily Dated
• "No-Call" List	• Easily Ignored
Electronic Mail	*Internet/Web Sites*
• Filterable	• Passive Content
• Becoming Over-used	• Regular Maintenance/Updating
• Contact Identification	• Provides Information to Competition
• Difficult to Gain Attention	• Ongoing Commitment

The more recent technology-based channels are also not without problems. Messages sent via e-mail can be filtered (and are rapidly being used almost to the point of saturation), obtaining a quality contact list can be difficult, and gaining quality attention can be problematic. Finally, Internet Web sites often require the intended target to initiate contact and, to be effective, these sites require an ongoing commitment to site maintenance and content monitoring. Taking into account both the positive and negative aspects of direct marketing channels, it becomes vitally important to focus on the keys to building an effective and efficient channel.

THE ROAD TO SUCCESS: POINTS TO PONDER

A review of our discussion reveals that, in the case of each of the four direct marketing channel options presented, building particular characteristics into the direct marketing channel strategy will put any firm, large or small, business-to-consumer or business-to-business oriented, on the right road to success.

As we have seen, success in telemarketing is neither advanced rocket science nor is it the adoption of an approach akin to a walking artillery barrage. Using the former perspective often means adopting a telemarketing strategy so data-heavy and complicated that to achieve anything reasonably close to success it would require an almost 100 percent "hit" rate. On the other hand, the later is built around a massive shotgun approach—the very quantity-over-quality paradigm that produces the results, and resulting stereotypes, of telemarketing that we are trying to overcome.

Figure 10-3 Keys to Direct Marketing Channels: The Matrix

Keys to Successful Direct Marketing Channels:
The Matrix

Telemarketing • Timing • Receptivity	*Direct Mail* • Targetability • Lasting Impact
Electronic Mail • Credibility • Relevance	*Internet/Web Sites* • User-Friendly • Value-Added Information

Successful telemarketing is founded on two simple principles: timing and receptivity. Earlier on we delved into the importance of understanding your consumers'(current and potential) behavior in the context of your firm and its offering. There are few places in which this knowledge is more practically valuable than in determining the best time to make a telemarketing contact. By understanding the times when your customers will have your offering foremost in their minds, you are far more likely to be successful contacting the customers, who (based on consumer behavior knowledge) the firm knows are more likely to be "hungry" for the product being offered.

At the same time, receptivity (an emphasis on quality over quantity in the actual message) is also necessary. Good telemarketers know exactly *what* they are going to say, *how* they are going to say it, and *why*. The proposed script, complete with various contingencies depending on the response given, is both the most vital and frequently overlooked key to successful telemarketing. InfoCision Management Group, a firm that started as a one-person company based in the owner's garage, has grown to be one of the country's leading telemarketing fundraising firms with a specialty in nonprofit and political organizations. The challenge of convincing a customer to be confident in establishing a value-for-value relationship is daunting enough; getting these same individuals to make a financial commitment for little or no personal gain, via the telephone, is in many ways unimaginable. Gary Taylor, the founder of InfoCision, credits his success to quality scripts that are extensively tested and practiced before they are actually used. Mr. Taylor's commitment to the importance of "scripting" is so deep that, to this day, he is still personally involved in script development and application.

Like telemarketing, the effectiveness of direct mail is also based on the proper use of consumer behavior knowledge. However, in the case of direct mail, this has less to do with the timing of the contact than it does the targetability of the contact. To put it simply: Put your direct mail materials into the hands of *quality* potential customers, not just anyone. This means searching your existing customer data for potential patterns as well as possibly moving outside and conducting primary market research. The other characteristic of effective direct mail is a long-recognized, yet often overlooked, characteristic—*lasting* impact. Well-targeted direct mail, containing a significant amount of product and firm information, will be kept as a resource by the customer for the future. Over a century ago, Sears & Roebuck understood this when they introduced the concept of the mail order catalog. Somehow that lesson has been lost over time by many firms and organizations.

In e-mail, one needs to take a "sniper" not a "shotgun" approach. Using e-mail means creating credibility and relevance. Credibility can be derived simply by (1) clearly identifying your organization and (2) sending the "mailing" out, no matter how large the targeted segment, in such a way to avoid the "spam" label. Our objective is "steak" not "spam" the recipient—don't make the recipient have to guess the source and don't try to cleverly hide the source of the contact. If you have applied your basic marketing principles, there should be at least a reasonable chance they *want* information about your organization and its offerings. Secondly, it is imperative that your offer is clear, obvious, and explicit. Every e-mail has a subject line. Use it just like a traditional advertisement would use a tagline—directly communicate your core message at the outset.

This brings us to the Internet/Web sites as a direct marketing channel. In effect, a good Web site incorporates some of the same characteristics of a good brick-and-mortar retail store. Specifically, a good Web site is user-friendly. That is, customers can easily access the information they are seeking. To that end, it is vital that any firm or organization using Web sites as part of a direct marketing channel should avoid the "tech-trap." It is undeniably true that the average Web site user is incredibly more sophisticated, technology-wise, than just a few years ago. At the same time, it is important to recognize that, no matter how enamored your information technology (IT) people are with the latest bells and whistles, your site should be an electronic map to your firm and it offerings—not a maze that requires time and effort to negotiate. Finally, recognize that by building such a site your organization becomes a *resource* that customers, and potential customers, will seek out again and again.

Perhaps the definitive example of the application of direct marketing principles in establishing an effective channel to customers, particularly using a Web site as the foundation, is Spits Bits. Spits Bits is essentially a one-man operation located in Northern California that supplies parts for Triumph Spitfire automobiles. Sold in the United States between the early 1960s and 1980, these cars were popular, sold well, and had a wide appeal among sports car enthusiasts. Unfortunately, like many British cars sold in this time frame, there were a number of model variants resulting in a wide variety of possible replacement parts. Not only does Spits Bits stock these parts, which can be ordered online, the company also provides extensive, detailed diagrams for virtually every aspect of the car that rival the original factory dealer workshop manuals. A customer can identify and purchase the exact part they need. After receipt, they can access the Web site to see how even the most minute or complex assembly fits together or alternatively they can contact the company directly for personal customer support. With its huge following in the United States, Spits Bits has achieved no small feat for a small specialty firm and provides a solid illustration of the power of a direct marketing channel.

SUMMARY

To summarize, let's consider the key lessons for constructing an effective direct marketing channel:

- Direct marketing channels are a means of accessing customers that are available to all sizes of firms and organizations.
- Using direct marketing enables firms to sidestep the issue of power/dependency in their channel strategy.
- A direct marketing channel affords the firm more direct control.
- Increased channel control leads to increased quality in customer relations and increased margins (i.e. revenue).
- Direct marketing channels provide a quick and efficient means to substantially expand a firm's markets.

Never forget that direct marketing channels are generally cost-effective options for firms and organizations of all types and sizes. Does that mean each is equally valuable or all should be considered? No. The answer as to which is appropriate for a given operation is predicated on a clear understanding of the organization's product offering, a solid knowledge of current and potential consumer behavior, and an awareness of the firm's strengths and weaknesses in terms of direct marketing expertise.

Direct marketing channels enable small to medium size firms not to only sidestep the problems of power and dependency associated with traditional marketing channels, but also it actually *empowers* these firms with much higher levels of control over their channel to the customer. This direct conduit to customers naturally leads to an increase in the quality of customer relations, which has a direct link to increased revenue. Finally, direct marketing channels enable even the smallest of firms to expand their market not only domestically but also internationally. In particular, e-mail messages and Web sites are by and large unencumbered by geographic boundaries. Just ask Nigel at Spit Bits. He might even pass along a decent recipe or two for no charge.

Chapter 11

FULFILLMENT AND SERVICE: MEETING AND EXCEEDING THE CUSTOMER'S EXPECTATIONS

Ann Daher Fleming and Linda M. Foley

> A customer is the immediate jewel of our souls. Him we flatter,
> him we feast, compliment, vote for, and will not contradict.
> —Ralph Waldo Emerson

Throughout history, the customer has always been cherished. It has been said, "the customer is king" and "the customer is always right." Customers always have been known as the lifeblood of every organization. However, we occasionally hear grim statistics, such as most Fortune 500 companies lose 50 percent of their customers every five years, the average company communicates only four times per year with customers and six times per year with prospects, and it costs 7 to 10 times more to acquire a new customer than it does to retain an existing customer. We have also found that a 5 percent increase in customer retention can increase profits 25 to 125 percent. So, why then do so few companies have databases to analyze customer satisfaction and retention? If you asked any random manager what the overall determinant of their customers' satisfaction and loyalty was, do you think they could answer you?

Unfortunately, it's a lot easier, quicker, and cheaper to examine numbers, such as profitability, sales, or even the number of times that each customer is contacted. Even the best manager simply cannot know how to please each customer, or even whether that should be a goal that needs to be achieved. Quite frankly, as customers, we all want different things and are all satisfied by different things.

There are diverse reasons to become loyal to a business, some of which are because the customer absolutely loves the business and is very emotional about it, and some reasons center on the fact that the business is simply closest to their home. Then, to complicate matters, if you did completely understand how to satisfy your customers, would you know how to communicate this wealth of knowledge to them? With the advent of information technology, including Web sites, e-mails, faxes, direct mail, and voicemails, there are a multitude of touch points to communicate with the customer. Although the original intention was to provide quick and easy access to information to improve customer satisfaction, it just does not always happen. Customers have been bombarded with too much information, especially with information that did not enhance the purchase of a company's product or service. In some cases, customers received conflicting information from a company's various communication vehicles. Consequently, customer satisfaction levels may have been reduced despite a company's attempt to increase customer satisfaction levels.

In addition to all the other factors that have complicated the vague concept of customer satisfaction, it is now more challenging for companies to determine the causes and influencers of customer satisfaction. Companies may evaluate customer satisfaction with one contact point, (once again, by stressing the numbers), but they may not evaluate the customers' experience that is the result of a company's collective effort. What did the customer feel like? Were they happy? Why were they happy? How did everyone in the company make you feel? For example, a company will send e-mail surveys to customers inquiring about customers' experiences with a company's Web site, but not inquire about the customers' experiences with the company's sales representative or the customers' impressions of their advertisement. This is an important point because customers form opinions on their total customer experience with a company. After all, we buy emotionally and defend logically. It's almost impossible to go back after the fact and ask a customer to break apart their experience into individual variables. You are either happy or you're not, but from a personal standpoint, you probably do not know exactly why.

Because customers speak in generalities, they are not specific or objective in their opinions about their customer experience with a company. For example, customers will say, "I'd never go back to Company A, they're a bunch of idiots. You should go to Company B; they will take good care of you." These types of general statements obviously damage a company's reputation. However, how will the company ever find out about it? If they do hear of it, how will they ever know who said it or why? If the business does not know that, they will never have the opportunity to improve its customer service performance.

UNDERSTANDING CUSTOMERS' NEEDS

So, the million dollar question is where, when, how, and why should you focus your efforts to gain, improve, or maintain customer satisfaction? But that question cannot be answered without understanding the need that the product or service is expected to fill as well as the expectations the customer has for its performance. Too often a company will launch direct marketing programs without doing any research on its potential impact to customer satisfaction. Meanwhile, they may heavily invest their marketing budgets to reach new customers. Without understanding the needs of these new customers, these companies are just flying blind. For example, some customers may rate a manufacturer's on-time delivery as poor, but they may still be satisfied with the quality of the product and continue to purchase it. The product quality meets the customer's needs and expectations despite the unreliable product delivery.

Although a company provides a high-quality product, they need to understand customer expectations and what drives customer satisfaction. This is especially important when a company is directly marketing to potential customers. For example, if the on-time delivery is important to these potential customers and the company's on-time delivery is unreliable, then all the money invested in attracting these new customers is at risk of being wasted if a company cannot produce acceptable product delivery for these new customers.

The retail industry knows the importance of providing superior customer service. In many cases, it is their competitive advantage. Nordstrom has enjoyed this advantage for many years. A study sponsored by both the National Retail Federation and American Express showed that 85 percent of consumers would shop more frequently and spend more at retailers that provided exceptional customer service.[1] Like retailers, manufacturers also strive to provide exceptional customer service. Because manufacturers have a diverse customer base with different needs, it is sometimes more difficult to define customer needs and expectations. Consider the following example.

A manufacturer collects customer feedback regarding their on-time delivery performance. Overall, their customers responded by rating this manufacturer's on-time delivery performance as inadequate. However, the manufacturer's internal metrics show that they meet their promised delivery date to customers at about 95 percent of the time. Why are customers not satisfied with this manufacturer's delivery performance? In an attempt to further explore this issue and uncover an opportunity to improve customer satisfaction ratings, the manufacturer launched a customer survey campaign to collect data on their on-time delivery performance. Some of the questions that they were trying to answer were as follows: What lead time on delivery do customers require? Are competitors offering more aggressive delivery dates? By reducing lead time, what type of business impact can the manufacturer expect to see?

Through this customer survey campaign, the manufacturer learned that customers required shorter lead times than what the manufacturer offered. Furthermore, the manufacturer also learned that the competition was able to provide significantly shorter lead times. Although the competition had shortcomings in other areas of its business, it did provide the lead times that customers desired. By gaining a better understanding of customers needs, this manufacturer was able to devise a fulfillment and service strategy that realigned its internal resources to reduce lead times, which ultimately led to higher customer satisfaction levels.

Therefore, it is essential that you understand what is important to your customers, both current and new, and then seek to align your resources and capabilities to meet your customers' expectations. The answer to this conundrum is relatively straightforward, but it is not easy or cheap to do. It is absolutely imperative to invest in top-notch market research to delve deeply into an understanding of customer satisfaction before moving on to the next step.

MEETING CUSTOMERS' CHANGING NEEDS

Meeting customer expectations retains a customer for one day. Exceeding customer expectations builds long-term customer loyalty, which is particularly important in the face of today's cut-throat competition. If most companies know this, then why aren't they actively gauging their customer's satisfaction level? Using customer satisfaction surveys on an ongoing basis can serve as a baseline for customer satisfaction. Rich survey data can be an early indicator of changes in the level of customers' satisfaction. This step, like the previous step, must be done carefully and correctly, because of the extreme importance of the information that is being gathered. An ongoing analysis is particularly important when faced with changing competitive tactics. The actions of your competitors may drive changes in customer satisfaction levels that you may not even be aware of because you have not changed anything about your own product or service. Collecting customer data and analyzing it on an ongoing basis provides the company with an opportunity to self-correct before customers become dissatisfied and reach the "point of no return." Ultimately, customer dissatisfaction leads to decreased or lost sales.

Using sales numbers as a single indicator of customer satisfaction does not provide the entire picture. Sales are sales—nothing more, nothing less. This becomes an even bigger issue when analyzing trends over time. When sales are stable from year to year, you may assume that your customers are relatively satisfied. Consider this example: A retailer of children's clothing has been purchasing the same amount of clothing from a certain manufacturer for years. The clothing store has been so successful for so many years that they decide to branch out into other lines of clothing. Having just received a catalog in the mail from a different manufacturer about their specialty women's clothing line, the retailer purchases an order from the new manufacturer. The retail store owner did so without even considering their present supplier. There was never anything wrong with the present supplier, and they continued to purchase the same or possibly even greater amounts of children's clothes. However, the original manufacturer did not invest money, time, or effort into determining whether or not the retailer's needs were changing. Thus, because they did not step in and send a catalog of their adult clothing, the manufacturer lost the opportunity to gain new business. Sales data would not have shown this need. You must go beyond what simple numbers say, and do this on a constant basis.

Think again about the previous example, but take it a step further. What would have happened if the current manufacturer exceeded the retailer's expectations by providing better on-time delivery, more responsive customer service, or a listing of their other or perhaps innovative new products? Investing time and money upfront in cultivating good relationships with current customers and understanding customer needs is more cost-effective then investing marketing funds in searching for new customers. This rule holds almost every time. As mentioned, it costs 7 to 10 times more money to get a new customer than to keep a current one. This concept is very straightforward. Think about yourself as a consumer. Which are you more likely to read: direct mail from someone that you have never heard of or direct mail from a company that you buy from regularly?

FULFILLMENT AND SERVICE STRATEGY

Smart direct marketers know that developing an understanding of customer expectations and how these expectations are changing is a key to success. Because this process is so critical, it cannot be done haphazardly, but instead, it must be preformed in a deliberate, strategic manner. A *fulfillment and service strategy* is based on understanding customer needs and expectations and delivering products and services to meet or exceed these needs and expectations. Companies that are successful with their fulfillment and service strategy understand that they first need to understand what drives customer satisfaction and then align company resources to produce the expected performance.

Customer satisfaction is the extent to which a product's or services' perceived performance matches a buyer's expectations. If product or service performance meets or exceeds a customer's expectations, then the customer is satisfied to some degree. Some companies collect data on their customer satisfaction ratings from their customers so that they can monitor their performance and adapt direct marketing programs to increase their customer satisfaction ratings. The key concept here is expectations. Do we receive the same level of service at a five-star restaurant as we receive at a fast-food restaurant? Do we even expect the same things? If you go into a fast-food restaurant, you do not expect someone to come by and clean up your mess. You expect to get up and take it to the garbage can yourself. In fact, if someone did come by and cleaned up after you, you would be shocked and amazed, in a good way. However, at the five-star restaurant, if none of your dishes were removed throughout the meal, you would be very upset at the end when you had a pyramid of appetizer, salad, entrée, and dessert plates stacked in the middle of the table.

It is all about expectations. We have different expectations from every single business before we walk in the door. If our expectations are met, we're satisfied, if our expectations are exceeded, we're ecstatic. The big hurdle that marketers usually do not recognize is that every time expectations are exceeded, the bar just got raised. Meaning, if you did go into a fast-food restaurant and someone was walking around cleaning up after everyone, you may begin to assume that this particular franchise really cares about cleanliness. If you went back and saw that a worker was once again cleaning the eating area, you would begin to expect it, possibly because you have become loyal to this location because of their attention to detail. Thus, what some marketers do not realize is that it is a lifelong process, and should be one of the bar continually being raised. Therefore, it is even more critical to constantly monitor customers' changing expectations throughout time. At first glance, this scenario might seem a bit daunting. Does this mean that every time someone walks through the door of my establishment I have to do better and better? In some ways, yes, but here is the wonderful news: Statistics show that every time a customer walks through the door, they also spend more money. As loyalty builds, total purchases increase. So, it is also necessary to understand profitability over time.

Excuse the very crude example, but it is really a lot like dating and relationships. How hard is it and how much effort do you need to put forth to find someone and get a first date? At that point, how much do you know about your date and understand his or her needs? How much reciprocity or "profitability" do you expect at this point? Maybe, if you are really lucky, you may get a hug. Then compare this to someone that has been dating for the long term. You expect more in terms of commitment, but you also allow for occasional slipups and are usually more forgiveness. There is also more and more "profitability" over time, unless, in all seriousness, both members of the couple are not feeling like they are getting more out of the relationship than what they put into it, in which case the relationship should end. The decision of when to "break up" will be discussed at the end of the chapter.

Relationships with customers are exactly the same. Long-term quality relationships produce greater outcomes than an infinite series of one-time customers. There is a different level and type of effort that needs to be expended, but it is definitely worth it when it comes to long-term profitability. Successful companies invest in a fulfillment and service strategy and implementation because they recognize the long-term value that a customer represents. The models for customer lifetime value and customer impact value quantify the revenue generated from customers.

The *customer lifetime value model* shows the entire revenue stream of purchases that the customer would make over a lifetime of patronage. The *customer impact value model* reveals the value of the entire stream of purchases that a single customer has generated for a company both directly and indirectly over a lifetime of patronage. It takes into consideration additional revenue streams generated by a customer's referrals.

SO, WHAT'S A CUSTOMER WORTH?

Particularly in the retail market, consumers are not differentiated from one another—all customers are treated the same. However, not all customers are the same. Some are more profitable than others. The profitable customers should be given special consideration, especially when they ask for it. But this does not always happen. Consider this impact under the customer lifetime value model.

The customer lifetime value model represents the entire revenue stream of purchases that a company would gain from a single customer's patronage. The customer lifetime value model is especially relevant to companies relying on customer referrals. Consider the following example. A drycleaner in the midwest provides dry-cleaning service to Mr. and Mrs. Smith. This couple has frequented this drycleaner on a weekly basis for the past seven years. They spend an average of $30 a week on their dry-cleaning services. On one occasion, the drycleaner misplaced the couple's dry-cleaning order of seven shirts. After 30 days, the drycleaner determined that the shirts were lost and could not be found. The drycleaner told the couple that they would reimburse them for replacement shirts at the same value of the lost shirts. The couple purchased the replacement shirts and presented this receipt to the drycleaner in anticipation of reimbursement. However, the drycleaner refused to reimburse the couple for the dollar amount because the couple had spent an average of $50 on a replacement shirt, which the drycleaner thought was excessive. The drycleaner normally reimburses at $30 per shirt but did not share this information with the customer. The total dollar discrepancy between what the customer expected and what the drycleaner wanted to pay was $140.

At the time that this occurred, the couple had already spent approximately $11,000 in dry-cleaning services over the course of seven years at this drycleaner. Because this was not taken into consideration when determining the amount to be reimbursed, the drycleaner refused to reimburse for the dollar discrepancy. Consequently, the couple decided to find another drycleaner. If the average life of a customer at this drycleaner is 15 years, then refusing to pay this $140 dollar discrepancy actually cost the drycleaner $12,570 in revenues over a period of the remaining eight years. Although the company policy is not to reimburse over $30, they should have realized that there are exceptions to every rule.

Similarly, the customer impact value model represents the entire revenue stream of purchases, both directly and indirectly, that a single customer has generated for a company over a lifetime of patronage. This model shows the impact of customer referrals. In other words, in the previous dry cleaning example, the business owner should have realized not only the potential to lose $12,570 over the next eight years, but also how much business would have been gained from all of the Smith's friends, relatives, and acquaintances had they reimbursed the expected amount—not to mention how much business would be adversely affected when, instead of the Smith's bragging about the drycleaner, they complained about the business. On average, we tell 10 people when we have a bad experience with a business and we tell only 1 person when we have a good experience. Some people, like teachers and doctors, tell as many as 20 to 100 people when they are dissatisfied. That fact is a little secret in the academic world. When professors get really upset with a business, we make sure to insert it as an example is every class every semester. There is one particularly bad story that one of us has about a large insurance company, and we have probably told more than 4,000 people to never do business with the firm. Then, once you figure in that some of those 4,000 people might have told a few of their friends, the numbers can really add up. Unfortunately, even as marketers, we don't use too many examples of great companies in our classes. It is simply just easier to complain than to brag, not to mention that it makes for a better story.

When we are talking about businesses that are close to our hearts, the impact of referrals becomes even greater. Parents often seek referrals from other parents before selecting the best school, preschool, or childcare services for their child because, after all, we are talking about trusting our greatest gifts in the hands of someone else. But just imagine that the following had happened: A new customer enrolled their baby into a preschool's full-day program. At the time of enrollment, the family was told that if they were to take a vacation that they would receive a 50 percent discount off one week's paid tuition. When the time came to take the vacation, the preschool realized that the family was not eligible for this quoted discount.

The preschool faced the decision of charging the family the full week's tuition, which would disappoint their customer, or honoring the quoted discount to meet their customer's expectation. The preschool honored their word. Rather than focusing on the revenue gained from one week's full tuition, they forgave the $150 discount because they realized that there was much more value to be gained by a satisfied customer in the long term. The customer lifetime value model and customer impact value model demonstrate this revenue gain from a current customer and the referrals generated by this customer.

With four years of preschool at an approximate rate of $60 per day and $15,600 a year, this customer's lifetime value amounted to $62,400. The customer impact value is based on the customer lifetime value plus additional revenue stream directly generated from its referral business. In this case, if the customer generates one additional customer with the same weekly schedule, then their customer impact value is approximately $125,000. Using the customer lifetime value model and customer impact model, this preschool can make better business decisions when deciding how it will meet its customer's expectations.

The drycleaner lost a customer because of their treatment of a $140 discrepancy, while the preschool choose to forego the $150 discrepancy and retain the customer valued at $62,400. A fulfillment and service strategy provides a company with a big picture view of what is important to the organization—*keeping good customers*. Companies can make better business decisions on their fulfillment and service strategy when they understand their customer's expectations, both spoken and unspoken.

The savvy direct marketer knows to ask, "where were the customers acquired?" What type of service have they come to expect? How well does the company's performance meet the customer's expectation? New customers with high expectation for service might be annoyed if the new company produces slower response rates then what the customers have been accustomed to. They would ask, "why can't you do it here?" The savvy direct marketer knows the importance of fulfilling unspoken needs and when it is appropriate to meet these needs.

Not all customers are the right match for a company's products and services. Some customers' expectations may not be easily satisfied with what the company can deliver. However, if a company is planning on acquiring new customers, then they should realize that acquiring new customers, especially if they are their competitor's customers, brings expectations that need to be recognized and addressed. Sometimes, meeting or exceeding these expectations is manageable. Other times, meeting these expectations is too costly for the company. The company must decide when it is appropriate to meet customer's expectations.

RECOGNIZING AN UNPROFITABLE CUSTOMER

Not all customers are good matches for a company. It has been said, "You can't be all things to all people." A low-cost provider better serves customers looking for the lowest possible price. A manufacturer of high-quality products and services is more successful at meeting the expectations of customers that value these attributes.

A couple went to a furniture store and purchased a recliner for their family room. They are the type of shoppers that like to find a great deal on high-quality goods. They proudly tell others about their purchases that they "got it for a steal." They managed to furnish their beautiful home with these types of goods found during their shopping treasure hunts. After multiple attempts to find the perfect recliner for their home, they managed to find the right style, quality, and comfort, at a great sale price according to the company's advertisement. However, this recliner was priced at about 30 percent higher price than what this couple wanted to pay for it. They kept nitpicking at the imperfections of the recliner and had the store pick it up for a replacement recliner three times over the course of two months. After the third attempt for a pickup, the retail store associate said, "Maybe you should shop somewhere else." Unless the price was reduced, this couple was never going to be satisfied with this purchase.

SALVAGING A GOOD CUSTOMER

A furniture dealer purchased large quantities of furniture direct from the manufacturer. When his sales slowed down, he attempted to take advantage of the manufacturer's return policy to continue to return the surplus of inventory. After his third attempt failed, the manufacturer's sales representative made a plea to have the company accept this inventory return. The sales representative knew of the long history with this high-sales-volume customer and did not want to jeopardize the business over this inventory return. The customer service manager at the company agreed to accept the inventory return based on the sales representative's request.

Six months later, the furniture dealer attempted to return more inventory. The customer service manager began to research the financials of the furniture dealer and learned that this customer had filed for chapter 11 bankruptcy. This customer was returning his inventory to reduce his debt. Realizing that the furniture dealer grew too fast and faced cash flow issues, the furniture manufacturer helped the customer with extended terms during their chapter 11 filings. Eventually, the furniture dealer moved out of chapter 11 and again became a profitable customer for the furniture manufacturer.

DIFFERENTIATING A GOOD CUSTOMER FROM A BAD CUSTOMER

Not all customers are bad customers. By understanding customer needs, a company can better differentiate a profitable customer from an unprofitable customer. This insight can help direct a company's focus on its fulfillment and service. How did the one store decide that the bargain-hunting couple was simply never going to be happy? How did the furniture manufacturer realize that the retailer would once again begin purchasing large quantities?

Unfortunately, there is no easy answer, and a lot of the answer comes from gut and intuition. The good news is that the ongoing analysis of customer needs through market research and an ongoing look at profitability and the customer value models can show a very revealing picture.

Chapter 12 delves into the measurement issue in a much deeper fashion, but as far as understanding needs, that is where direct marketing is critical. If you are trying to reach a customer, which approach is more effective: (1) running a television ad without any knowledge of your customer, where they are, what channel they are watching, if they are flipping passed the commercials, or whether they are even watching at all, or (2) sending them an e-mail or giving them a phone call when you know the e-mail address is correct and you know, based on their lifestyle, that they are probably interested in your product? Neither method is foolproof, but you obviously will have much better odds with the second approach. Thus, if you are trying to determine and or manage your customer expectations to decide whether or not they are a profitable customer, no method is more basic, simple, and direct than asking them. Have you ever tried to figure out what a friend is thinking? Have you ever overanalyzed something to a point beyond confusion, when you know the simplest thing to do is just to ask the question? We generally do not ask, however, because of various reasons, like time and anxiety. However, in regards to customers and money, there is no excuse for not doing your best. You simply have to connect with them directly—with the caveat of doing it correctly.

HOW DIRECT MARKETING MESSAGES CAN IMPACT EXPECTATIONS

Direct marketing programs that generate information that is not valued by customers can be wasteful, at best, and ultimately can lead to lost customers. Misaligned direct marketing programs are a constant reminder that the company does not understand customer needs. Most customers understand what junk mail is and typically receive it at home. Customers begin to think, "they know me so little." After all, even being well versed in all the topics of direct marketing, we still open my mail over the garbage can and ignore incoming calls from "private" or "unknown" numbers. This type of situation has the same result in a business environment. Consider the following examples that demonstrate the difference in receptiveness from direct mail recipients.

They Know Me So Little

A midwestern manufacturer sells its products directly to distributors. They manufacture more than 5,000 products and serve more than four distinctly different market segments with a customer base of 20,000 distributors. Although their customers are in distinctly different market segments, the company chooses to conduct mass mailings to all their customers with the same marketing pieces. This is a costly endeavor. Conducting mass mailings to a general audience, without targeting the audience, not only increases the direct cost of the mailing, but also has an impact on those recipients that receive the unintended mailing. When a mailing is too general and not well thought out, it sends the message directly to the customer base that the company does not recognize customer needs. The customer's impression of the company is that "they know me so little."

Consider the following example of sending an unintended message to customers. A car owner services his vehicle at an automotive dealership on a regular basis. This consumer services the car according to the recommended schedule from the automotive manufacturer. On more than one occasion, the consumer serviced the car at the automotive dealership and paid full price for the services rendered. One week later, this consumer received a direct mail brochure with several coupons from the automotive dealership where his car was just serviced. After the second time that this occurred, the consumer became upset when he realized how much money he could have saved if he would have received the coupons in advance of the services. The ramifications of the ill will generated by this direct mailing are hard to measure. If the customer becomes upset enough, he may look for another service provider.

They Know Me So Well

Most consumers who move into a new house are looking for local resources close to their home. They are looking for a local doctor, dentist, hair salon, insurance agent, and so on. For a short period of time, these types of consumers are desperately seeking new services. However, this time period is relatively short lived. Once they get accustomed to their new surroundings and start meeting new people, it will no longer be the "desperate" search for services. Thus, for local service companies looking to acquire new customers, it is advantageous to market to customers just as they are relocating.

A direct mail campaign targeted at these customers at the time that they are searching for a new provider is not only timely, but also can prove to be effective. Consider the welcome wagon package that is mailed to potential customers when they move into their new home. Both the provider and consumer are seeking to develop a relationship. Here is a golden opportunity to acquire new customers by connecting with the right customers at the right time. But even this great example is not always handled very well. Usually, marketers pay to have their advertisement or coupon included within the welcome wagon packet and then never follow up.

After a recent move, one of us can remember selecting the coupons that applied to services that might be needed and putting them in a pile in the corner of the desk, with plans to come back to them at a later date. However, as time passed in unpacking boxes and getting used to the new city, more papers piled up on that stack. A few months later, while cleaning, the entire stack got picked up and thrown away. It was just sitting there collecting dust. Just imagine how much more impact the coupon would have had if, for example, a carpet cleaning company had called to inquire whether the carpets had been cleaned yet. Potential customers would not have to take time out of their day to locate a company and then call a number; they might say no, I have not, and ask how much the company charged. Direct marketers need to develop a complete understanding of their customers. Not just what their possible needs might be, but also how they go about ordering the service, what their needs are at the time they are using or receiving the service, and what their needs are after the service has been delivered. It's a complete circle—one that never ends.

In this circle, timing is everything. Companies should realize that their direct marketing efforts directly affect their ability to meet or exceed their customers' expectations. With the example of the automotive dealership, the dealership should time their coupon mailing to be mailed before the recommended schedule or should only mail the coupons to customers that are delinquent with the manufacturer's schedule. Mailing a welcome wagon package at the time that consumers are receptive to this service proves to be an effective direct marketing tool.

DIRECT MARKETING THROUGH LOYAL CUSTOMERS

Astute direct marketers know that, for the long-term success of their companies, they need to meet their customers' expectations to retain customers in the long term and ultimately convert them into loyal customers. They achieve this through a fulfillment and service strategy. They know that loyal customers provide many benefits to a company in the long term, including the following:

- More loyalty and less defection to the competition
- Lower acquisition costs and longer retention rates
- New referrals by word of mouth

Converting customers into loyal customers has many long-term benefits for companies. These benefits include an effective marketing tool in acquiring new customers and an open relationship in which these loyal customers provide valuable information for companies to improve the quality of their customer service. Using your loyal customers as a key marketing tool is one of the best direct marketing tools available. After all, what is cheaper and more credible than a personal referral?

Parents often solicit other parent's advice on recommendations for schools in an informal manner. A midwestern high school for girls recognized this trend and formally pulled these two groups together at an event promoted as "Coffee Night," at which the high school matches a prospective group of parents that have something in common with another group of parents whose children are already attending the school. Then one of the parents whose daughters are currently enrolled in the high school hosts the "Coffee Night" at one of their houses. One of the matching variables may be, for example, that they may have sent their daughters to the same elementary school. Because the two groups share something in common, the prospective group of parents is more likely to connect with the other group. Then, because of this connection, the prospective group of parents may feel that the group of parents whose children presently attend the school are a more credible source to ask questions about the school. This high school has found that these "Coffee Night" events yield a great return on their marketing investment. Their advertising and direct mail efforts created awareness among their target market, but it is their loyal customers that helped them close the sale.

CUSTOMER LOYALTY AS A DEFENSE TOOL

Loyal customers will align themselves with the company even during the most competitive times. Why wait until then to discover who these customers are? A true test of a customer's loyalty is when the competition specifically targets these customers with aggressive direct marketing programs and they still choose to stay with you.

It is typical practice in the software industry to have a one-year contract with clients. A midwestern software consulting service offers a software management service to its customers on an ongoing basis. Their price is about 10 percent greater than other software service providers. Despite their higher pricing, this software consulting service is able to maintain customers through excellent customer service.

As the competitive market became more intense, the competition started to target this software consulting service's customer base. They determined that in order to avoid an annual bidding war with its competition that they would lock their customers into a longer contract period to reduce the opportunity for the competition to steal their customers. They created a new format for contract periods. They were the first in their local market to launch a 36-month term contract, which offered its customers a 10 percent price reduction if they signed up. With their new contract terms, this software consulting service was able to successfully retain their customers over a three-year period and reduced their time in bidding wars. By doing so, they redirected their efforts to continue to serve their customers well.

BUILDING CUSTOMER LOYALTY

Should companies invest their direct marketing dollars exclusively in acquiring new customers? Or should they expand their focus to include servicing existing customers? Retaining customers through good customer service can prove to be effective in many businesses, particularly when the company is service oriented.

A group of small business owners meets monthly for the Lake County's Entrepreneur Club. Six business owners representing various industries, including seafood distribution, copy machine distribution, and machine parts repair, were asked why they thought they had high customer retention. Despite the differences among the industries, they responded with the same answers:

- Understood their customer needs
- Regularly communicated with the customer
- Reliably and consistently delivered what was promised to the customer

Meeting customers' expectations consistently and reliably builds customer loyalty in the long term. Not only will loyal customers maintain their relationship with their current provider, but also they most likely will help generate new referrals for their provider. Then, business will continue to grow.

SUMMARY

Successful companies know the value of a customer. They understand their customers' business needs and challenges. They devise a fulfillment and service strategy that guides their overall decision making in servicing their customers and recognize that it is tool. These companies know that how they fulfill one customer's needs maybe different from how they fulfill another customer's needs. They are familiar with each customer's unique situations and know when it is necessary to be flexible with their fulfillment and service program.

Successful companies are also aware that the fulfillment service strategy must adapt to their customers' changing needs. These companies stay close with their customers to understand their customers' business opportunities and challenges. They align their fulfillment and service offerings to maximize opportunities for their customers. Most important, successful companies know that their focus should not be exclusively on acquiring new customers but also on retaining customers through their fulfillment and service strategy.

Keep in mind the following guidelines:

- Understand customers' expectations and what drives customer satisfaction
- Understand how the company influences customer satisfaction through its fulfillment and service
- Recognize good customers and when it is necessary to provide special fulfillment and service to these customers
- Strive to build loyal customers so that they maintain their tenure with the company and generate new referrals
- Recognize when customers' needs have changed and adapt the fulfillment and service offerings to account for these changes

Chapter 12

MEASUREMENT AND ASSESSMENT: ANALYZING AND INTERPRETING PERFORMANCE RESULTS

Ann Daher Fleming and Linda M. Foley

> A right result, at this time, will be worth more to the world, than ten times the men, and ten times the money.
>
> —Abraham Lincoln

It has been said that the definition of insanity is doing the same thing over and over again and each time expecting a different result. Well, marketers must be a bunch of insane people, because day in and day out they repeat the same efforts and invest the same amounts of money with the continued expectations that somehow, someday, sales will go up. An even more daunting thought is that usually, when business owners do make the decision to redirect their efforts, they usually do so because of a random thought or because their "gut" tells them to do so. Unfortunately, just as the other saying goes, "It takes money to make money," or in other words, you have absolutely, positively got to invest time and money in a thorough and complete measurement and assessment system before making business decisions. You simply cannot make an educated, well-informed decision about changing the direction of your company before you have developed a deep understanding of the business, the business environment, and all the variables that are producing the cause-effect relationships between money invested and sales or profitability outcomes.

However, there is some really good news here too. As a direct marketer you have it easier than all other types of marketers to analyze your performance. One of the buzzwords of today is ROI (return on investment). Everyone wants to know, for every dollar they put in, how much are they getting out? Imagine being an advertising executive. They have perhaps one of the hardest tasks when determining ROI. They know exactly how much money they spent to run a certain advertisement, but how can you relate that perfectly to sales increases? Maybe your advertisement was so bad that it actually would have caused sales to go down, but your main competitor went out of business so your sales went up. This example is of course oversimplified, but the facts remain that there are an infinite number of things that can happen between point A (buying advertising space) and point B (increase in sales). Likewise, imagine the task of relating something even more indirect, like public relations efforts or money invested in sports sponsorships to sales. If people hear good things about your company, like, they do good things for the environment, or if customers are more familiar with your product because there was a sign on the score board at a baseball game, will that translate into increased profitability? How would you ever know?

Which brings us back to the good news: Although this task is still daunting and complex for direct marketers, it is much easier. When you connect directly with your customers, you know their immediate reaction. Personal selling and direct marketing are the only two marketing communications elements that share this tremendous advantage. It's pretty obvious to analyze the result when a customer hangs up the phone on a telemarketer. This part is easy, but what is necessary to stop the "insanity" is to figure out why the customer hung up the phone. Were they not interested in the product? Was the telemarketer rude? Did they not use the right sales pitch? The exactness of the how's and why's is where this chapter comes into play. It is essential for a business owner to determine these factors.

MEASUREMENT AND ASSESSMENT

The true test of a plan, regardless of how thoughtfully developed and executed, is its delivery and performance. Such a system helps create a stronger understanding of what caused success and failures in the past. Thus, with this knowledge, direct marketers can better design and launch more effective direct marketing programs and yield a higher ROI. Measurement is not a new discipline to organizations. It has always been employed but driven by a different source. Traditionally, measurement systems have been constructed and calculated by finance managers under the direction of company executives. These metrics are limited in their scope for marketing—they gauge the progress of sales, customers, and profitability. They do not measure performance results for a specific direct marketing program. Do direct marketers know which programs produce the greatest ROI? Therein lies the opportunity. By developing metrics to measure results from direct marketing programs, a direct marketer can choose the best investment option.

Without understanding what caused the performance of a direct marketing program—what happened or why it happened—the cycle can only repeat itself if the results were bad and only hope that it repeats itself if the results were good. When the results are favorable, the direct marketer focuses on maintaining activities that may have contributed to the results. When the results are unfavorable, the direct marketer launches a new marketing program in hopes of reversing the situation. When the marketing program yields lackluster results, the direct marketer may launch another new direct marketing program. Or, they may drastically reduce marketing budgets all together, without realizing the impact on an effective direct marketing program.

A systematic approach to analyzing performance can help avoid these situations. By assessing the performance of each direct marketing program, a direct marketer can better understand the contribution that the program makes to the business. Measurement and assessment is an essential tool for direct marketers in revealing the factors and influences that distinguish a successful direct marketing program from the rest. It is not black magic. It is a discipline that involves time and effort in establishing a measurement and assessment system with a solid understanding of what happened and why it happened, and, most important, how the success can be repeated with future direct marketing programs.

For the direct marketer, the benefits of measurement and assessment include the following:

- Recognize direct marketing techniques that worked, did not work, and the driving forces behind the results
- Gauge progress toward reaching direct marketing goals
- Detect early signs of issues that may detract from the goal
- Maximize return on marketing investment
- Compare competing direct marketing programs for investment options

A measurement and assessment system is more effective in gauging progress when multiple metrics are used and when their relationship to one another is understood. For example, an organization measuring its customer defection rate in comparison with its customer retention rate recognizes that sudden changes in results deem further investigation. Capitalizing on opportunities or reducing issues are some of the benefits of a measurement and assessment system.

LEVERAGING INFORMATION

Measurement and assessment alone is not effective. It is not enough to collect data or even to have a measurement system that tracks the progress. The real value comes from knowing what to do with the data and how to leverage that information into a direct marketing program that is right for its customers at the right time. Ever place an order with a mail order catalog company such as Lillian Vernon or Omaha Steaks? After placing the order, they will ask customers whether they want to hear about "today's specials" or place a repeat order for something that may have bought from them previously. Amazon.com also employs the same techniques with books. These companies capture the opportunity for an additional sale immediately.

Another example of establishing a relationship with customers is often employed by baby diaper and food manufacturers. They collect information from soon-to-be mothers and mail appropriate size products for the baby during each phase of development. They further encourage dialogue with their customer base through Web sites and phone. It is not coincidental that when the baby reaches one year in age the parent receives the next size diaper, brochures on a child's development, coupons for toddler food, or portrait coupons from photographers.

While some organizations have had years of experience in developing their direct marketing programs and establishing a measurement and assessment system, most organizations have not reached this threshold. It requires discipline, time, and investment. Other organizations can benefit by enhancing their "analytic intelligence" in establishing appropriate metrics that truly measure meaningful outcomes. Analytic intelligence means not only developing the right metrics, but also understanding the inputs and outputs of the measurement system and the factors that influence the process. It is avoiding myopia and taking a holistic viewpoint.

A measurement and assessment system is made up of metrics that track performance. The key to accurately assess progress is to develop the right set of metrics. For example, consider people that are looking to improve their health. What metrics would they use to measure progress? If they were attempting to reduce their cholesterol level, would a weight scale provide the proper metric in tracking cholesterol levels? It may have a slight correlation, but it certainly would not be the best indicator. If the same person were attempting to lose weight, would a heart stress test show that they were taking the right steps to achieve their goals? Once again, it would be close and highly correlated, but it should not be measuring the same thing.

Metrics represent data points that can be used to assess progress toward a goal. Metrics are the data points and performance indicators for key activities and outcomes. They set expectations and measure progress. As goals change, metrics need to be adapted. As mentioned, it is critical that the correct metrics are used to assess each individual problem or issue.

The *measurement system* is the employment of a systematic process in which a group of metrics is analyzed. Each metric is considered on the basis of its own merit and in relationship to the others to determine performance results. Consider a consumer that follows a strict low-fat diet every day, receives counseling and support once a week, and exercises five times a week. This measurement system is most likely to be employed to measure a desired outcome rather than to measure progress based on a single metric. In this instance, weight, body mass index, cholesterol, and other indicators should be used together to determine progress.

Assessment is the interpretation of the results. It is a comparison of the results to some other measure, which includes program goals, other similar programs, or other industry standards. Performance results are compared with another set of data or with goals to gauge progress—this is a *baseline*. Baselines can represent data from a previous time period or forecasted metrics. In some cases, a *benchmark* is established. A benchmark is like a baseline in that it compares data. This data are compared to an industry standard or to the results of an admired company. Benchmarking is especially useful because, whether we want to admit it or not, nobody is perfect in all things. Thus, even a giant like Wal-Mart could gain from the use of benchmarking. For example, while many businesses look to Wal-Mart for logistics advice, Wal-Mart would gain by benchmarking someone else in terms of social responsibility or human resource management.

MEASURING AND INTERPRETING PERFORMANCE RESULTS

The primary purpose of a measurement system is to generate actionable information that can be used to aid a manager in making better business decisions. What type of information will lead to better insight into the greatest return on the direct marketing investment? A measurement system should measure important activities that directly relate to the success or failure of a direct marketing program.

Direct marketing programs can be designed to directly impact these performance indicators. Consider a direct marketing initiative that captures more leads than what is typical, but the conversion rate from qualified leads to new customers remains the same. A significant increase in the leads captured is good news. However, not being able to translate the qualified leads into new customers leaves unanswered questions for a direct marketer. Was this increase from truly qualified leads or simply from people looking for a free offer? A measurement system will highlight this opportunity. An astute direct marketing manager will recognize this opportunity to learn why the conversion rate remains untouched. Was there an influx of leads that were not followed up? Were the leads improperly qualified as potential customers? Was there a change in the market conditions that caused the customers to lose interest?

HIDDEN OPPORTUNITY

Consider this scenario. A direct marketer walks down the office hallway and crosses paths with his organization's president or the president approaches him in the lunchroom to ask, "how's business doing?" Does he provide her with the standard answer, "business is good," and wonder why she continues to probe as he tries to dart into the restroom or shove his sandwich into his mouth? The president is really looking for a newsworthy headline. Presidents of organizations want to know what is going on that makes for an exciting front-page headline. "Business is good" is not a cover story and implies that, although sales indeed might be good, that he really does not understand what is driving that business condition or, worse yet, that he is not maximizing the business opportunity. Imagine the excitement of creating a newsworthy headline worth talking about in the office. What if this newsworthy headline was easily in reach? With direct marketing, there are two key areas to reach and subsequently measure: retention and penetration.

RETENTION: KEEPING YOUR CUSTOMERS

A manufacturer of consumer equipment collects and stores warranty card information submitted by consumers. Previously, warranty cards were only used by the customer service department when servicing customer or product issues. Through the years, they collected information on customers, including the type of product purchased, date of purchase, and mailing addresses. Knowing that their customers purchased a replacement product every three years, they knew when their existing customers would be potential customers for a replacement product.

When the direct marketer analyzed the customer warranty databases, she realized that more than 12,000 customers made their last purchase $2^1/_2$ years ago and most likely would be purchasing a replacement product within the next 6 to 12 months. She designed and launched a direct marketing campaign targeted at these 12,000 customers. The campaign consisted of direct mail kits that contained a customer service telephone number for product information. More than 8 percent of those direct mail recipients called the customer service department for product information and a total of 4 percent direct mail recipients immediately purchased their replacement product. Thus, through a relatively simple assessment (building a list of the customers that had not purchased recently) and because of the average order size of $3,000 from the 480 customers who reordered, this campaign generated approximately $1.4 million. And that assessment probably took less than an hour and almost no money.

RETENTION: RECOGNIZING OPPORTUNITY

A large architectural firm in the midwest specializes in interior design for commercial buildings. They cultivate relationships with real estate representatives that bring them new clients. The architect meets with new clients to learn of their working style then creates an interior design that best meets his or her client's needs. The firm's efforts are primarily focused on acquiring new clients through real estate representatives. After they service the clients, they do not retain the relationship with them during the length of the lease. Consequently, when the client's lease has expired or if they have decided to move to another location, the architectural firm may miss out on following their clients to their new location and miss the opportunity to establish a relationship with the new tenant. Imagine how different this scenario could be if the architect maintained and analyzed a database of his customers. One of the worst mistakes that marketers can make is pouring all their time and effort into gaining new customers. Retaining old customers is sometimes just a matter of keeping good records, knowing what and when the customers will need new products, and then using a relatively simple direct marketing method to reach them and determine if they are ready to reorder.

PENETRATION: MINING HIDDEN OPPORTUNITY

Competent data analysis can also create opportunities for cross-selling and up-selling. A major manufacturer of consumer goods sells equipment through distributors. This manufacturer offers several products that are grouped into product categories. After measuring and analyzing customer sales, they realized that 20,000 customers purchased from some of their product categories but did not select complimentary or related products from other product categories. For example, these customers bought consumable products used with this equipment from other manufacturers—their competitors. Why would they purchase their consumable products from multiple manufacturers? Was there an awareness issue? Was there an opportunity to capture these sales?

The opportunity to increase sales was noted. The direct marketer launched an e-mail campaign that was targeted to reach those 20,000 customers. With more than a 2 percent response rate, 400 customers demonstrated interest in learning more about their consumable products. Of the 400 interested customers, 80 of those customers converted from their original supplier to this company as their new supplier. With each customer buying more than 10 units per week, they collectively represent a sales increase of 41,600 units per year. Consider the residual impact of this program in the long term. This analysis was slightly more complex. Not only did the manufacturer need to track sales, but also they needed to conduct some cross-referencing. However, the results still definitely make it worth the time and effort. Now, just imagine if the manufacturer had taken it a step further and instituted a market research campaign aimed at determining consumer attitudes. Data analysis would have pinpointed answers to these earlier questions. The following example describes this benefit of data analysis.

PENETRATION: UNDERSTANDING CUSTOMER NEEDS

An insurance agent was trying to penetrate his existing noncommercial accounts through direct mail. He evaluated his client services and identified services not used. He then created a personalized letter to his clients identifying other services available for purchase. He mailed the personalized letters along with an enclosed response card with the option of learning more about the additional programs. His main purpose was to generate interest and gain permission for follow-up, but at the same time, this effort was giving him a chance to identify what other services might be of interest to his noncommercial accounts. With assessment, this insurance agent was able to identify new sales opportunities and measure the efforts through a direct mail campaign. But, more important, once he obtained permission to make follow-up phone calls, he could ask the consumers more about their needs. This, once again, is an advantage of direct marketing that does not exist with any other type of marketing communication, with the possible exception of personal selling.

All these cases show that direct marketing programs can be very effective in acquiring new customers, retaining old customers, or penetrating existing accounts deeper, all in the effort to eventually increase sales. Understanding why direct marketing programs are effective is important when developing new programs and investing funds. Consider the president approaching the direct marketer in the hallway or in the lunchroom with the proposition to double their marketing budget if they could more than double the results. Should the direct marketer take the offer? What should he do with the money? Should he invest it into a single direct marketing program or should he divide the funds among several direct marketing programs? The benefit of measurement and assessment provides information to determine the most effective program for investment. What if you had done your analysis and became fairly confident that you could double your sales with a direct marketing campaign? Just imagine if you could go to the president and say, "If you double my budget, I will double sales!"

CAUSE-AND-EFFECT RELATIONSHIPS

Measurement and assessment can provide a direct link between a direct marketing activity and its result. This link can prove that direct marketing activities deliver results. It is like a "cause-and-effect" relationship. There is an outcome to every direct marketing activity and an opportunity to produce a desirable result. To achieve such a result, a direct marketer needs to create a direct marketing plan with a strategy, goals, and supporting programs. A measurement and assessment system lets the direct marketer know whether they are on course to achieve the desired results. Most important, it provides a lesson on how to design effective direct marketing programs that have the potential to improve performance that can be evaluated for its full contribution.

Measuring e-Mail Campaigns

With an e-mail campaign, there are several metrics that could be used to assess performance. Consider the total number of e-mails sent, number of e-mails opened, number of visitors to a company's Web site, and number of customers that requested a product demonstration by a company representative. Additional information can then continue to be collected, like return visits to the site, which can be monitored through cookies and/or IP (Internet protocol) addresses. Also, companies can see and examine the time of the day, day of week, and month of the year that the visits were made and even see features about the user's computer hardware, software, and Internet service, all of which have their unique advantages depending on the type of product you are selling.

Consider expanding the focus to include sales activities that directly resulted from this e-mail campaign. For instance, a midwestern manufacturer of plumbing equipment utilizes e-mail campaigns to increase awareness and generate qualified leads for their sales representatives. In one of their e-mail campaigns that was targeted at consumers, e-mails were sent to 24,245 consumers and 8,632 e-mails were opened by consumers, 1,136 consumers clicked through to the company's main Web site. At the company's Web site, a total of 303 consumers requested a follow-up product demonstration from the company's sales representative. By only generating 303 qualified leads or with only 1 percent of the e-mail recipients requesting follow-up, the e-mail campaign results do not appear to be impressive. However, with a product price of $4,000 and 303 qualified leads, this e-mail campaign generated more than $1 million for the company. Likewise, return visits to the site had been noticed by many of those that had not yet purchased. Thus, a second and possibly third wave of mailings to those who seemed interested might net even more gains. Evaluating only the e-mail activity without considering its impact on sales can lead to incorrect conclusions.

Measuring Direct Mail Campaigns

With a direct mail campaign, tracking and measuring the number of recipients who responded is a typical metric. For example, a producer of a new sparkling wine is launching a direct mail campaign targeted to known champagne consumers. The producer mails direct mailers with a $5 off coupon to 100,000 targeted customers and received an immediate response of 5 percent. Thus, because

5 percent of the customers from the original mailing of 100,000 purchased a bottle of champagne at $20 a bottle, the producer increased their sales by $75,000 (assuming only one bottle per customer). However, continual measurement and tracking is just as necessary as the initial measurement. Once a database has been developed, a customer who was concerted into a buyer from the initial mailing could be tracked because this information would be available.

So, to further assess the value that this direct marketing program generated, consider what happened after the direct mail campaign was over. Of the 5,000 recipients who purchased the champagne with their $5 off coupon, 2,000 customers became regular customers and purchased it four times per year, and 1,000 customers became occasional customers and purchased it once a year. For a $20 bottle of champagne, this translates into an $180,000 sales revenue increase that does not link back to the direct mail campaign. Most important, this is an incremental increase in the sales revenue stream. In less than two years, these newly acquired customers will generate more than $250,000 in sales. The immediate sales generated by the direct mail campaign at $75,000 were measured; but by not evaluating the residual impact, the real impact of the program was underestimated.[1]

Measuring Events

Imagine assessing the performance of an event. What should be measured? First measure each "critical touch point" that the customer has in engaging with the company. By measuring and capturing this type of information, a baseline can be created to compare the results from one event to a similar event. As a pattern is established, and multiple variables are measured, you can begin to focus more on measuring those key activities that have the biggest impact on results. Assessing why one program may deliver different results is an important learning opportunity that could be applied to maximize performance of future programs.

The following key metrics will provide valuable information in assessing the performance of events:

- Cost per Contact: Divide the entire program investment by the gross number of contacts generated.
- Cost per Visitor Reached: Divide program cost by the number of potential prospects who visited the booth. Cost per visitor for the industry average ranges from $116 to $195, according to the

Exhibits Survey, Inc.[2] The focus should be on attracting the right prospects and customers to the booth.

- Cost per Qualified Lead: Divide total program cost by the number of qualified leads generated (includes leads that have not yet been qualified). Provides the opportunity to compare the results of one event to another event. Can determine the value of each program when evaluating for a marketing investment.

- Expense to Revenue Ratio (E:R): Divide the total revenue associated with the business event by the total expense incurred. This is a widely used metric for marketing communications. Some companies use E:R thresholds that may range from 2.5 percent to 5 percent to control spending.

Making the connection between a direct marketing program and a sale can be very challenging, particularly in those situations in which there is a long selling cycle or when there are multiple engagements with the prospect before a sale is captured. For a cost comparison, consider using an E:R ratio for these situations because it provides a more realistic comparison than other metrics, including ROI. Likewise, pipeline analysis provided by most CRM (Customer Relationship Management) software packages provides very rich detail. Pipeline analysis is an examination of a sale as it goes through the "pipeline" from lead to a sale. This type of information is critical to determine how long a customer takes to decide to purchase, how many contacts need to be made for the sale, and even points in which the customer can be easily "turned off."

This new way of looking at data as the entire pipeline and not just two points—a lead and a sale—is critical. Consider mapping the customer's touch points with every engagement with the organization. By mapping touch points, direct marketers can identify areas that they want to measure to gain a better understanding of how they affect customers' buying experiences.

Following are touch points for customer solicitation:

- Prospective leads
- Qualified leads
- Request for proposals
- Web site activity
- Coupon redemption
- New trial buyers
- Customer acquisition
- Customer conversion from lead to first time buyer

Following are touch points for customer life:

- Customer conversion from first time buyer to repeat buyer
- Average life of customer
- Customer lifetime value
- Average customer order size
- Referrals generated
- Customer complaints
- Customer compliments

Following are touch points for customer retention:

- Customer defection
- Customer reactivation

ANALYSIS AND INTERPRETATION

In addition to data gathering, great analysis and interpretation must be in place. Once again, sales are sales—nothing more, nothing less. Yes, you have to have the data before you can do anything with it, but once you have the data, you must know what to do with it. This provides the real news—the reasons why the numbers are up or down. Think of the Dow Jones reporting unusually high or low numbers. The numbers are reported in one sentence. Then they quickly move on to what drove the change in the numbers and then discuss what the possible drivers of the results were. Being able to distill the results down to what they mean for the organization's key metrics is important. Like a journalist, a direct marketer needs to understand what drives the numbers, what is driving the outcome, and how to maintain progress or implement change.

Yesterday's News: What Happened?

Understanding what happened and why it happened is the first step toward creating an effective direct marketing program with results that can be repeated. A measurement and assessment system can help direct marketers get there. Its performance indicators will warn them when trouble is ahead or reaffirm them if they are on course to reach their goals. Without a measurement and assessment system, direct marketers leave the results to chance.

Employing a "flying by the seat of your pants" approach is a risky proposition because business decisions are based on untested assumptions. Gambling with one's own money for sport is one thing, but taking unnecessary risks by gambling with the organization's money is irresponsible. Gambling can leave one vulnerable to experiencing significant unexpected results or surprises. With serendipity, a direct marketer wonders how it happened and if it is repeatable. With regret, a direct marketer dwells on what caused the dismal results and how it went unforeseen. In both cases, the outcome is not good because the direct marketer has not learned what caused the result. Therefore, they could neither repeat nor avoid the outcome in the future.

One Metric Does Not Fit All

A midwestern training facility has 10 years of experience of successfully training computer professionals. With sales stabilizing, they want to further grow their sales revenue by adding training for business professionals. They created a 30-page catalog of training classes for computer professionals and business professionals. They mailed 10,000 catalogs and received a 2 percent response rate in which a combination of 200 business and computer professionals registered for training for the year. They thought that 2 percent was a good metric to use because that is an industry standard. During the course of the year, classes were being conducted at half capacity and just breaking even while other classes were cancelled because of a lack of interest.

Although 2 percent is widely known as a good benchmark for a response rate on a direct mail campaign, it does not apply to all situations. With the combination of creating, printing, and mailing catalogs as well as administrative costs, they spent $250,000 on their catalog mailing. If their average student spent at least $1,250 during the course of the year, then they may break even. They did not have metrics against which to measure the results, so they did not realize that the response rate was not enough to sustain them. It is not only about compiling the data, but also about the integration of that data. Integration means bringing together various bits of information to help complete the picture. This step is key. Communication of various departments helps with this integration.

Communication as Part of Success

A company that manufacturers and markets musical instruments has its manufacturing facility and operations management located in one area of the country, while the marketing offices are located in the opposite part of the country. The direct marketing department creates a new 20-page color product brochure with the intensions of launching a direct marketing campaign to increase market awareness on existing products for the following calendar year. She mails the direct marketing pieces by the end of November to get a head start on the following year. Within a few weeks of mailing the direct marketing pieces, the direct marketer notices a sharp increase in sales. However, over a couple of weeks she notices that the gap between booked orders and shipped orders starts to widen past the acceptable quoted delivery time. The direct marketer becomes concerned and contacts the operations director to learn why there is a delivery issue. Could it be that demand exceeded supply? Was there a shortage of raw materials? Was there a human resource supply issue?

Unbeknownst to the direct marketer, the operations director intentionally reduced inventory levels, including raw material with long lead times, during the last two months of the year to avoid any inventory surpluses at year-end. There was a major communication problem and, more important, there was no alignment of goals. If the direct marketer and operations director would have aligned their goals initially, the direct marketer could have achieved her sales goals while the operations director could have reduced his inventory for year-end.

DISTINGUISHING CAUSE-AND-EFFECT RELATIONSHIPS

In both examples, there was not a connection between direct marketing activities and the goals that they were supposed to support. With the training facility, they did not define their metrics and did not measure and track its performance. With the music company, they did not align their goals within the organization, so they lacked organizational support in reaching their targeted metrics.

Remember to do the following:

- Communicate the direct marketing plan to the team
- Define program goals and objectives and align them with the organizational goals and objectives
- Design direct marketing programs that will help obtain targeted goals
- Create metrics to measure progress toward reaching the goals
- Measure and assess the performance on a timely basis to make mid-course adjustments

Yesterday's News: Why Did It Happen?

Answering the question "why did it happen?" can be a daunting task if there is a wide gap on the metrics between performance targets and results, especially when the metrics are reporting lackluster results. These types of events are referred to as variances, both favorable and unfavorable.

Analyzing and determining what drove the result can be subjective. It is important to collect supporting evidence that points to the same conclusion. The real test is determining the key drivers to isolate and control the variance to determine its true impact. For example, if sales increase by 20 percent on a single product during a 30-day period, did the finance department launch a special one-time financing program? Did customer service run a sales contest among its sales representatives? Or, did an unforeseen event occur? Did the competitors temporarily run short on inventory? Did the sales force land the first order of a major house account? Although there is a lot of up-front work in developing the knowledge and understanding of the influential factors that can affect results, the payoff is the opportunity to make midcourse adjustments to meet performance expectations.

SUMMARY

Astute direct marketers know that a measurement and assessment system is an essential tool that provides them with valuable information for decision making. Which direct marketing programs yield the highest ROI? Is the direct marketing program on track with meeting expectations? Which changes to the direct marketing program produce the most significant improvement to outcomes? When should changes be made to improve results? What factors can influence the success or failure of a direct marketing program?

When budgets are shrinking and performance expectations are rising, a measurement and assessment system can provide insight into those direct marketing programs that are most likely to produce the greatest return on the marketing investment. Over time, a measurement and assessment system may also provide valuable information that could be used to create performance expectations for new direct marketing programs—the type of results to expect and the timing of those results. The following guidelines must be used when employing a measurement and assessment system:

- Develop an understanding of cause-and-effect relationships
- Build analytic intelligence by creating metrics that measure meaningful outcomes
- Gauge progress of a direct marketing program with its goals
- Understand the factors that significantly impact the outcomes of direct marketing programs
- Compare direct marketing programs to one another to identify programs that provide high ROI
- Integrate and never stop revising

Chapter 13

ADAPTATION AND INNOVATION: MODIFYING AND CHANGING DIRECT MARKETING PROCESSES

Linda M. Foley

> You have no choice but to operate in a world shaped by ... the
> information revolution. There are two options: adapt or die.
> —Andrew S. Grove

Most of us understand that innovation and adaptability are crucial
elements to success in today's business environments. The ability to
change, learn, and innovate faster than your competitor clearly
shows a strong positive effect on performance. Innovativeness allows
companies to account for market uncertainties and enables companies to stand apart from their competitors. Yet, most companies are
simply falling short in terms of both adaptability and innovation. The
idea of being innovative seems to fall somewhere between a cliché
catch phrase and an illusive prescription from academics preaching
for firms to become learning organizations.

The big pharmaceutical firms are becoming more and more
aware of the consequences of the hypercompetitive markets and the
constant need for innovations and product differentiation. The pace
of "fast-followers" has accelerated and the time between innovation
and second-generation products has dropped from years to
months—and even in some cases weeks. Pharmaceutical companies
spend more than $1 billion annually on research and development
(R&D) and are coming under intense pressure to innovate. Additionally, they are finding it harder to maintain a price premium for innovative drugs. Insurers are becoming more reluctant to pay the high

prices for innovative drugs and are threatening to limit reimbursement levels.

One adaptation that the pharmaceutical firms have made is to change from mass-marketed advertising to a more direct marketing approach. D-T-C (Direct-to-Consumer) advertising has grown by 208 percent in the pharmaceuticals industry. What is remarkable about this is that the drug industry is so highly regulated that they are not allowed to conduct the same types of consumer research that typical companies can conduct and do not even have the same tools at their disposal to create successful direct marketing programs. Imagine beginning a direct marketing program with no consumer database and no legal ability to build such a database. The pharmaceutical companies have some information, but obviously they cannot keep tabs on every American citizen, what drugs they take, and their family medical history. This would be an ethical nightmare. Thus, the D-T-C approach is innovative and risky and has so far shown tremendous success rates. Just imagine what kind of growth could occur in non-regulated industries that employ direct marketing strategies.

It is not a difficult case to make that innovation is important to business owners. When "innovation" is searched on Amazon.com, a staggering 12,530 books are returned (as of January 2006, by the time you are reading this book, it has certainly increased). Thus, we are well aware of its importance. Yet, as one takes a quick perusal through the titles on Amazon.com, it quickly becomes apparent how little we actually know about innovation. Is innovation an application of R&D? Or, is innovation some form of organizational culture that, when applied, leads to more innovativeness or greater creativity? Does it involve the hiring of and empowerment of great, diverse employees? Is it a form of organizational learning or the management of computer information systems? What about entrepreneurship? Does entrepreneurship lead to innovation or vice versa?

The answer to these questions lies somewhere in the middle. Innovation is and can be all of the above. Yet, given that we know the importance of innovation and adaptability, it is very strange that it is declining, especially in America. Companies spent less on R&D in the third and fourth quarters of 2005 than in previous quarters, which some suspect was to increase short-term stockholder gains. Even academic research has been declining. According to a recent *Fortune* magazine article, America is now second to Western Europe in terms of articles published in scholarly journals across all disciplines. Even an R&D giant like GE cut 1,000 research projects down to 20 in 2004.[1]

So, how can all these facts be reconciled? We know the innovation is important, we know it is a highly researched topic, we know

the benefits that it can provide (especially in a direct marketing context), and yet it is declining. The answer probably lies somewhere in
the previously described confusion about the concept of innovation.
Thus, the first topic in this chapter will provide a better definition
and conceptualization of the terms innovation and adaptability. Likewise, the paths to innovation and adaptability are outlined. More
specifically, this chapter focuses on the innovation and adaptation
within the context of direct marketing. Direct marketing itself is
likely to be one of the biggest innovations to which companies must
adapt. It has become apparent that mass marketing, as we know it,
is dying. Long gone are the days when running one advertisement
on the "big-three" television channels during prime time could generate a response. The total number of television ads necessary to
generate the same response these days is closer to 171. Thus, it is
critical that marketers adapt all their marketing efforts to the new,
fragmented, highly technical, and savvier consumers. As this book
has thus far demonstrated, direct marketing is *the key tool* of the
future to achieve greater response rates and higher levels of success
from marketing initiatives. Thus, the use of direct marketing itself is
innovative.

Of course, the implementation of a successful marketing program must follow an entirely new and innovative path. Gone are the
days of traditional telemarketing and direct mail. Direct marketing
must be entirely complex and technologically advanced. The use of
direct marketing can allow for innovative initiatives throughout a
company. Many feel that Google has revolutionized the advertising
industry. Advertisers only pay when their ads (or searches) are
clicked. The more that companies spend on their ads, or listings, the
more likely their listings are to appear on searches. Also, the more
carefully they define their product attributes, the more likely the consumer will be able to find their products online. This innovation in
direct marketing provides Google with more than $1 billion annually
in total revenues. However, even more potential for success lies in
Yahoo!'s approach to brand-building. Unlike Google, they have consistently required users to sign up for services. Thus, Yahoo! has
been building a massive customer database for the last decade. In
2000, most felt that Yahoo! was all but dead, however, with their
direct approach, they will likely prosper for a long time.

SO, WHAT EXACTLY IS INNOVATION?

True adaptation and innovation, which becomes a part of the
overall strategic intent of the company, is very different from a

simple bright idea for an advertising campaign. The ability to be innovative must become a solid and *consistent part of a firm's strategy and its overall culture*. This type of culture requires some very different elements. An analysis of "corporate culture" can become vague, so this chapter focuses on actual marketing processes. This ambiguity in fuzzy cultural terms instead of actual business processes is probably the source of most of the confusion. After all, what really matters at the end of the day? If you are a manager in a company trying to determine your next day's objectives, it has to be something you can actually *do*. Thus, although innovation and adaptability are a part of a firm's strategy and culture, becoming innovative can be described as a set of processes that can be enacted to produce greater creativity and, most important, the willingness and ability to change—on a daily basis.

Given that innovation is a broad term, this chapter breaks it down into two main types: *adaptive innovation* (also referred to as adaptive learning or adaptive change), which utilizes and modifies existing knowledge, and *generative innovation* (also referred to as learning or change), which is the learning process that involves the pursuit of new knowledge. Both types are equally important and no one is more important than the other, but there are some variations depending on the type of industry. These variations are described in the following sections.

Generative Innovation

A discussion of generative innovation is probably easier to discuss initially because it is at the extreme end of a continuum from doing nothing to doing everything. Imagine this: You are the once great IBM, but you are now trying to compete with Microsoft. Is there any hope of Lotus Notes taking Microsoft Outlook head on? Ed Brill, an executive at IBM, started his own blog (www.edbrill.com). He receives an average of 16,000 hits a day from customers around every part of the globe. These customers log in at every hour of the day and night to spread positive word-of-mouth about IBM's product or perhaps even make a complaint. Does this not sound all that impressive and innovative? Brill essentially has 16,000 customer surveys handed to him every day—for free. Now that's direct market research![2]

Generative learning involves doing entirely new things. It involves creating breakthrough products and processes. It involves challenging the status quo and being willing to take any kind of necessary risk. Innovation involves the same kind of risk and reward trade-offs that exist when investing your own money. If you decide to take a high risk and invest in international stocks, there is more reward potential. On the other hand, being conservative and investing money in a savings account involves almost no risk, but it also has a very small reward. Thus, managers interested in achieving generative innovation must be fully willing to accept the possible risk. Just think, everyone thought Dell was crazy at the thought of a direct PC company, especially with competitors like IBM and Compaq, but look at where they all are now. Likewise, Microsoft's and Southwest Airline's business models contradicted the previous thinking that market share leads to success. Instead, although they eventually gained market share, they were originally only concerned with driving up market growth rates. These types of radical ideas are perfect examples of generative learning and innovation.

In the book *Change or Die: How to Transform Your Organization from the Inside Out* by M. David Dealy and Andrew R. Thomas, the authors discuss the need to manage risk and reward creativity.[3] After managers determine that something needs to be changed (see Dealy and Thomas 2006 for a lengthy discussion), they must then realize some truths about creativity, risk, and change. Organizations must make room for the inevitable failure that will come from allowing and encouraging creativity. This is not necessarily bad, because success usually leads to complacency, which usually leads to failure. A good manager knows that some failure will happen and some success will happen. The key is to understand when to make a move, what failures are acceptable, and which ones are harmful.

A manager must never lose sight of the true internal and external realities. If you know your product and your company, and know that both of these are good, risk and change should never be detrimental. Pfizer has actually gone against conventional wisdom and has sent out direct mailers to both doctors and patients. What is unconventional about these mailers is that instead of raving about the products, the mailers mainly discuss drug risks. Why would a company do this? According to Pfizer executives, this method encourages doctor-patient dialogue. To take this approach, you have to be confident that you have a good product, and Pfizer is.[4] Yes, it presents a risk to purposely bring up product faults. This makes inherent sense because the product is a drug, so to the average reader this simply seems like the ethical thing to do. However, imagine how it seemed the first time product marketers offered warranties and satisfaction guarantees. After all, isn't the product so good that a customer would not need a guarantee? The successful marketer knows that there will be failures, both in terms of product failures and internal failures. However, these failures are good, because they tell you where to improve, and more important, the failures keep the manager from becoming complacent.

In addition to knowing your product and yourself very well, a good manager also understands the external realities. Giant Eagle, a supermarket retailer with stores throughout western Pennsylvania, Ohio, West Virginia, and Maryland, has always had a watchful eye on Wal-Mart and knows that it is nearly impossible to compete with the buying power of such a large retailer. However, also understanding the environment and the ever-increasing gas prices, Giant Eagle saw an opportunity. Although it is a completely new approach to think of a grocery store selling gas, store owners knew that a radical approach was necessary to compete with the likes of Wal-Mart. Thus, Giant Eagle began opening and operating gas stations and also enacting their own reward program in the store. For every $50 that a customer spends on groceries in the store, they save $0.10 on every gallon of gas. Because I drive an SUV and have a 90-mile round-trip commute, Giant Eagle has converted me completely. I have not shopped in a Wal-Mart in close to a year now. That is impressive transformation considering I used to go to Wal-Mart once a week. The transformation was based on two efforts on the part of Giant Eagle: generative innovation and direct marketing. In short, if you know your company and your products and services *and* understand the external environment and competitors, risk and even failure are good things, which must be managed not avoided.

Adaptive Innovation

While many grocery stores started using loyalty cards years ago, few have actually utilized them in the best way possible considering the enormous benefits that they can provide direct marketers. Although some may be offended by the practice of "selling" customer information, Giant Eagle has utilized the information obtained from the loyalty cards in a very beneficial fashion. Through the direct approach of gathering and analyzing information and having a direct partnership with Kimberly-Clark, both partners have gained. When a customer at Giant Eagle who regularly purchases size 3 diapers begins to purchase size 4 diapers, of any brand, notice is sent to Kimberly-Clark, the makers of Huggies brand diapers. Subsequently, the same customer is sent the Huggies brand size 4 diapers along with coupons for both the diapers and other products that Kimberly-Clark makes that are age appropriate for the typical weight of a baby wearing size 4 diapers. Thus, Kimberly-Clark gains by hopefully converting a Pampers user to Huggies or by selling additional

Kimberly-Clark products, and Giant Eagle gains by having the customer come back and purchase more in their store. This example is not quite as radical as the example of Giant Eagle selling gas. It is simply an example of a company taking their preexisting direct marketing efforts and modifying or enhancing these efforts to produce more beneficial results.

Adaptive innovation involves minor, incremental changes. It is the exploitation of things already known. *Boston* and *Philadelphia* magazines are two regional magazines that decided to take a fresh approach to magazine renewals. The old renewal notices looked "stodgy." Thus, instead of going to the internal creativity department, the magazine went outside to a direct marketing company for a completely new view. Instead of boring, black-and-whites notices that had text resembling, "buy now, save money," they wanted to make the renewal notices more like the magazine and "remind the readers why they liked the magazine in the first place."[5] The new notices used color and contained sample top 10 best restaurant lists along with other features common to the magazine. The results were quite impressive; subscriptions renewals were up 15.2 percent the next month.

To be adaptive, the extreme levels of change and risk as described previously are not required. Being adaptive is more about seeing small, minor internal or external shifts or changes and then subsequently making small adjustments to those changes. It is about realizing that innovation is not just radical, brand new products, but also anything that adds additional value in the customer's eyes. Adaptive innovation occurs when a company makes new network contacts. For example, when a home owner's insurance company partners with a home security company. Neither one of them do anything radically different, except for the fact that when the home owners receive their paperwork, they are not only told that they can receive a discount for getting a home security system, but also are provided with a brochure and a coupon for installation from the local security company.

Also, adaptive changes occur when a manager looks at their current customers and how they find out about their products. When Step 2, a local company manufacturing durable children's toys realized the word-of-mouth power that exists among moms, they started selling their products to daycare centers and preschools at a 20 percent discount. It was simply a matter of realizing that short-term loss in profits was negligible in comparison with the increase in positive word-of-mouth advertising.

Adaptive changes can also occur when a manager examines how their employees work and how things can be changed so that the employees work better. Smart Office Solutions, a business-to-business provider of multiple communications and software solutions, installed a new software system for their employees to use while conducting their daily telemarketing activities. The software provides an icon in the lower corner of each sales person's computer screen that resembles a gas gauge. The gauge approaches the "full mark" as the employee comes closer to reaching their sales goal for the day. Using this simple software implementation, they have increased sales by significantly increasing motivation. Thus, being adaptive is a matter of looking for the minor changes that can be made that will have an effect on how business is done or how the customer views the product. Adaptive changes are made as the day-to-day internal and external environmental scanning is conducted and slight discrepancies are noted. Basically, it is taking on the mind-set of looking for every single way possible to improve the company.

WHEN SHOULD YOU USE EACH TYPE OF INNOVATION?

The short answer to the question of when to use each type of innovation is that both adaptive and generative innovations need to be used at all times. To increase value in the customer's eyes, a firm must always pay attention to the small, incremental changes that need to be made to improve the product or the company's operating procedures. Omaha Steaks has found (as many marketers have found) that they can no longer reach customers through the once-standard process of bill-stuffed advertisements now that 35 million households pay their bills online. As the industry has changed, so has Omaha Steaks. They no longer include ads for their products in various consumer bills, which were costing them $0.04 to $0.05 per piece. They have instead opted to have their ads, along with their Web address printed on the back of ATM receipts.[6] These minor, incremental changes are necessary on a constant and consistent basis in any company.

Additionally, the consequences of generative changes are also something else that the marketer must always keep in mind. Even with slight daily improvements, markets and environments change significantly from time to time. Large breakthroughs become necessary to keep up with changing consumer needs or marketplace conditions. Thus, both types of innovation are necessary. The exact balance between the two types differs from company to company and cannot be determined exactly. However, based on the industry in which the firm operates, certain assessments can be made.

In a recent industry-wide study of many large companies, some of which were Fortune 500 companies, the following effects were found.[7] *Adaptive learning produced larger effects* and was correlated with growth strategy and organizational growth. Meaning, adaptive learning was actually more important for overall organizational growth in creativity, customer satisfaction, market share, and financial performance. However, the effects were different based on the industry. *Generative learning was highly correlated with environmental turbulence.* Thus, in this study, using and modifying existing knowledge was more beneficial to organizational financial growth than generating new knowledge, except in turbulent environments. So, if you are in a turbulent environment, like the computer software industry, generative learning is more important. In almost all other situations, although both types of learning should exist, the scale should be slightly more heavily weighted toward adaptive learning.

Even though most people think this logic sounds backwards, in that the breakthrough innovations should lead to greater results, the same study produced some insight into why this finding exists. The more mature and stable an environment is, the more likely it is for customers to be loyal. Brand loyalty can take an extremely long time to build and has many more variables associated with it, such as involvement and identification. Thus, dramatically changing a product can destroy previously established customer loyalty. The perfect example of this (of which almost everyone is aware) is when Coca-Cola changed their formula to New Coke. All the taste tests showed that consumers really did prefer the taste of New Coke, and yet when it was launched, it was a complete failure and was eventually pulled from the market. This is a perfect illustration of the fact that people were not buying Coke just for the taste; they were buying Coke for the total loyalty experience. Thus, the final lesson of this chapter is that both adaptive and generative innovation must be balanced to some degree, with a greater emphasis being placed on adaptive innovation unless it is a highly turbulent environment. Too much generative change can erode consumer loyalty.

SUMMARY

As Jack Welch, retired CEO of General Electric, stated, "Continuous learning is the key to success."[8] The principle of adaptability can be traced back 2,500 years in the literature to Sun Tzu, who stated:

> If a general is ignorant of the principle of adaptability, he must not be
> entrusted with a position of authority. The skillful employer of men
> will employ the wise man, the brave man, the covetous man, and the

stupid man. For the wise man delights in establishing his merit, the brave man likes to show his courage in action, the covetous man is quick at seizing advantages, and the stupid man has no fear of death.[9]

In this chapter, the following points have been discussed:

- Innovation is critical to success
- Direct marketing itself is an innovation
- Innovativeness must be consistent in mission and reflected in all aspects of organizational culture
- There are two paths to innovation: adaptive and generative learning

Generative learning involves breakthrough, that is, radical changes in both products and processes. It can lead to high returns, but also brings with it high risk. Risk must be managed and creativity must be rewarded. A manager that is well aware of their external and internal realities is best equipped to make decisions regarding both the return and risk potential of new projects. Adaptive learning involves minor, incremental changes. It leads to moderate, but more certain returns. It does not entail the same level of risk management and can also protect valuable customer loyalty. The two forms must be balanced to achieve the best possible results. Given that many marketers are still stuck in the traditional and outdated mind-set of direct marketing, the act of establishing a successful direct marketing program can lead to enormous profit potential and, by itself, can be an innovation.

Chapter 14

ETHICS AND PROFESSIONALISM

Steven Brubaker and Timothy J. Wilkinson

> Without commonly shared and widely entrenched moral values
> and obligations, neither the law, nor democratic government,
> nor even the market economy will function properly.
>
> —Václav Havel

Look out! Ryan A. Swanberg is out to get you. The following
appeared in *Direct Magazine*:

> If your business does direct marketing of any sort, stop reading this
> and check your database immediately to see if it contains the name
> Ryan A. Swanberg. If it does, purge his file pronto. Why? Because he's
> out to get you.
>
> For the past four years or so, Swanberg has made a decent
> living—about $100,000 annually—out of suing telemarketers and debt
> collectors who cross his path that in any way violate laws like the Tele-
> phone Consumer Protection Act, either inadvertently or on purpose.
>
> The 25-year-old, a high school dropout, makes no apologies for his
> admittedly unorthodox "career path"—the lawsuits are his main, and
> in fact only, source of income—and he has written a book about his
> adventures, *Lawsuit: How I Turned the Tables on Telemarketers and
> Debt Collectors....*
>
> By late 2001, Swanberg owed more than $25,000 on about 10 sep-
> arate credit cards, so naturally he was getting calls from debt collec-
> tors. One was so abusive he thought he might have a legal case against
> the caller. He did, and won, but the settlement was nowhere near what
> he had been promised by his attorney.
>
> Realizing he might come upon other such opportunities, and dis-
> gusted by the legal profession, he decided to teach himself about the
> law. Eventually, realizing the economic potential of turning his new-
> found talents on the telemarketing business, he made that a target. His

sights were so keenly trained on telemarketing that he even installed additional phone lines to boost the volume of incoming calls, and went out of his way to get on as many databases as possible.

Most of his cases are settled out of court, and he doesn't discuss specifics because of confidentiality agreements. Representing himself, he claims to have settled more than 60 cases with debt collectors and more than 200 with telemarketers, with the average settlement falling between $1,500 and $2,000.

Swanberg makes no distinctions between the big players and little mom-and-pop operations in his efforts, reasoning that if they break the law, they break the law. But he does say that he's accepted things like vacations, cell phone service, and carpet replacements as settlements in some cases.

As of the book's writing, Swanberg said he was involved in 20 to 30 lawsuits and multiple settlements, and had litigated more than 300 cases representing himself. . . .

Still, he's giving the world of respectability a shot. He's formed a consultancy, Swanberg & Associates, and is offering his services to debt collection agencies and telemarketing companies that want to train their employees on the proper procedures to avoid lawsuits. He doesn't have any clients yet, but several debt collection firms are interested.

[In a phone interview, Swanberg explained that] the goal in going public with his "career" in the book was both to educate consumers about how to protect themselves, and marketers on what they're doing wrong. . . . He openly admits that when telemarketers call him, he tests them to see whether they trip up.

"It's up to them to comply with the law," he said.[1]

This case illustrates the precarious path that today's sales organizations may end up on if they pursue direct marketing efforts without fully understanding their ethical and legal obligations. The telemarketing business, which is so often accused of taking advantage of others, has now become a victim. The problem is that the direct marketing industry is widely thought of as slimy, dishonest, money grubbing, and shameless. Just as advertising was perceived negatively during the early twentieth century, direct marketing receives that same judgment from many today. But just as the image of advertising changed over the course of a few short years, so too can the image of direct marketing. The key to this change is the professionalization of the field, with a focus on ethics and social responsibility at its core. You can avoid the Mr. Swanbergs of this world if you make the adoption and enforcement of high ethical standards a priority.

This chapter focuses on practical planning tools and processes that organizations can use to incorporate ethics into their operations for dealing with customer relationships. We briefly present the moral case for and against direct marketing and then provide five suggestions about how you can create an ethical direct marketing organization. Regulatory issues are also discussed.

THE ETHICS OF DIRECT MARKETING

John and Suzanne Morse have explained that the ethical case for direct marketing is based on the mutual benefits that are received by both the marketer and the consumer.[2] First, the firm benefits by not wasting scarce resources on marketing to disinterested individuals or firms. Traditional marketing either disperses time, effort, and money toward people who are not interested in purchasing the product, or it expends resources on accurately identifying the appropriate target market. Inefficiency always leads to higher prices and/or lower shareholder value. Second, through appropriate data analysis, the customer benefits by receiving less clutter (i.e., junk mail, pop-up ads, unwanted phone solicitations) in favor of marketing approaches based on the potential customer's income, interests, past purchases, and other relevant information. Direct marketing therefore increases efficiency by serving the interests of both the producer and the consumer.

The argument against direct marketing is that it is essentially an intrusion on an individual's privacy. Even if overall economic gains result from appropriately targeted marketing efforts, the cost is a loss of privacy to the extent that either (1) an individual is observed without knowing that he or she is being watched (e.g., cookies functioning without a computer user's knowledge or permission) or (2) an individual changes his or her behavior because of the knowledge that he or she is being observed. For example, a person might not visit a particular Web site if she realizes that tracking software will be automatically downloaded onto her personal computer. In either case, the violation of privacy that occurs outweighs the utilitarian value of the economic exchange that may result from direct marketing.

It is helpful to note that people who respond favorably to direct marketing efforts are more likely to be concerned about how firms use their personal information. They tend to believe that companies should limit the amount of information collected from customers and should not provide customer lists to other firms or organization without prior notice.[3] The direct marketer is therefore constrained by the ethical imperative to respect the privacy of potential customers. By observing respect for privacy as a guiding principle, firms can enjoy the economic and efficiency benefits of direct marketing while maintaining their moral, ethical, and legal responsibilities. As Pat Kachura, the senior vice president for ethics and consumer affairs at the Direct Marketing Association (DMA) states, "If a consumer doesn't want to get mail from you, you need to honor that. If they are 'privacy fundamentalists' they will not be responsive to your offer. If they want to find out how you got their name, you need to help them."[4] Striking a balance between the business imperative to create an effective direct marketing strategy while respecting the privacy of potential customers requires planning, leadership, and a corporate culture in which value is placed on high moral and ethical standards.

In the next section we provide a list of recommendations that you can use to create an ethical direct marketing business.

DEMONSTRATE LEADERSHIP AND MORAL COURAGE

The first step in creating an ethical business environment for your direct marketing efforts is to decide that you and your organization will believe in, and adhere to, high standards. The tone is set from the top. It is up to the leaders of a company to create both the strategy and the boundaries through which a business achieves sustainable competitive advantage. Unless the management team makes a conscious and ongoing commitment to high ethical standards, the firm will drift to the lowest common denominator in the organization, regardless of pithy sayings on wall plaques or ethics tips in company newsletters.

Whether or not they are aware of it, the CEO and his or her team communicate a moral vision. The firm president who has little interest in ethical standards and pushes an agenda of sales at any cost, will infect his employees with his amoral approach. Executives and managers lead by example. If ethics is important, managers must participate in ethics training or related events alongside firm employees. Managers must not only do the right things, but they must also speak the right language. For example, Jim, the manager of a large Midwestern direct mail company, regularly sent employees to mandated sexual harassment training and even made a show of attending these sessions himself. At the same time he tolerated and even participated in the crude jokes and discussions of several of the firm's senior vice presidents. As a result, his employees did not take the sexual harassment training seriously. Even after several lawsuits were threatened, this behavior persisted around the office.

Remember, 90 percent of leadership is communicated through the actions that you demonstrate to your employees day in and day out.

Leadership and moral courage displayed at the early stages of difficult or controversial issues will help avoid trouble later in the process. For example, an initial problem that took place when "predictive dialers" (automatic dialing) were introduced was that people would answer their phones only to be hung up on after a few seconds. Because of this technological glitch, many customers thought they were being stalked or harassed. According to DMA Senior Vice President Pat Kachura, the probability of this happening was discussed at an early meeting of the big players in the industry. However, no action was taken to reduce this negative and clearly predictable outcome. As Kachura states, "It doesn't make sense to make the quick buck today and ruin your reputation for the long term. If the president is not talking about the importance of doing the right things on a regular basis, there will be a real problem."[5]

ADOPT STANDARDS

To operate in a legal and ethical manner, you must set and enforce standards throughout your company. Fortunately, the DMA has produced a thorough set of guidelines that are available for adoption. They are designed to foster good consumer and community relationships and to protect direct marketers from potential legal problems. By formally adopting these guidelines and by seeing to it that they are put into effect, you are taking a big step toward protecting your firm from litigation. The DMA guidelines cover a wide range of topics, including the terms of the offer, advance consent in marketing, marketing to children, special offers and claims, sweepstakes and order fulfillment. Many of these guidelines reflect common sense: "Direct marketers should offer merchandise only when it is on hand or when there is a reasonable expectation of its timely receipt."[6] Other suggestions are less obvious: "The number, retail value (of non-cash prizes) and complete description of all prizes offered, and whether cash may be awarded instead of merchandise ... [and] the timing of payments."[7]

Implementing clearly defined standards is analogous to engaging in risk management to lower insurance costs. For ethical statements to be more than just words on paper, management must be self-conscious in the implementation of its ethical standards throughout the firm through specific actions. DMA guidelines are available on the association's Web site.

HIRE THE RIGHT PEOPLE

The best way to ensure ethical behavior among employees is to hire individuals with a sense of personal morality and responsibility. In addition to appropriate technical qualifications, the screening of applicants should include ethical criteria. We suggest that potential employees be rated on items such as trustworthiness, honesty, personal responsibility, and integrity. Assessing these characteristics is the challenge. Fortunately technological solutions are available that are designed to create personality profiles for applicants that can match personality dimensions to the requirements of the job. In addition, electronic screening of applications can detect red flags, such as misrepresentations or misleading information on resumes.[8]

CREATING AN ETHICAL CULTURE

After hiring the right people, the best way to encourage an ethical environment is through the creation and nurturing of an ethical corporate culture. A culture in which ethical practice is the norm can result only from ongoing vigilance and attention by executives and line managers. In their report, *Creating and Maintaining an Ethical Corporate Climate*, the Woodstock Theological Center states that the role of a firm's leadership cannot be overstated.[9] Rather than imposing standards by external edict, an ethical culture works best when it results from consensus and shared commitment. Such a culture is fashioned through explicit rules and informal norms that alternately reward and punish, honor and dishonor individual actions.

Jill, a stay-at-home mother of four, answered a sales call from a representative of Company A and asked to be taken off the company's calling list. The next week she received another call from the same firm. After getting the call center manager on the phone she demanded to know why they were calling after she had explicitly asked to be taken off the firm's list. The manager patiently explained that her name had been removed from the list that was used the previous week. However, the company was now calling from a new list that had just been purchased. He then claimed that the company did not have the capability to remove names from the new list. It was only later that Jill learned that the manager's explanation was not truthful. In fact, the ability to create and use a "suppression file" is uncomplicated and can be easily managed by even the most rudimentary telemarketing operation. In this instance, the problem was not with the firm's leadership (which had already adopted a code of ethics), but rather was the result of a lack of follow-through. Management had failed to disseminate its high standards throughout the organization.

DIRECT MARKETING LANDMINES

In addition to ethical concerns, managers face many compliance risks. These are ethical risks that have been codified into law. What follows are some of the most common (and dangerous) landmines confronting direct marketers and some steps that can be taken to avoid stepping in the wrong place.

Do Not Call List

By now everyone has heard of the Do Not Call (DNC) list, right? Wrong! According to the Federal Trade Commission (FTC), FMFG, Inc., a Nevada bed company, made two years' worth (900,000 or more) of illegal phone calls to consumers who had registered with the DNC list. This firm had called potential customers falsely claiming that they were taking a poll about people's sleeping habits. While legitimate surveys are exempted from the DNC list, fake surveys are illegal under the DNC legislation.[10]

The DNC covers all calls made to solicit consumers or sell goods through interstate phone calls. Calls from political organizations, legitimate telephone surveyors (where no sales pitch is included in the call), charities, or calls from companies with which a customer already has a business relationship are exempt. However, third-party telemarketing on behalf of charities is subject to the provisions of the DMC list. Direct marketers must access the DNC registry and update their calling list every 31 days. Compliance with DNC requirements is basic for firms that wish to avoid unpleasant entanglements with the FTC.[11]

Racial Bias

You may have seen news reports of an attorney general's office investigating a mortgage company because of racially biased lending practices. In most cases though, mortgage and lending institutions represent one of the best models for Equal Housing Lender and ethical business practices. The culprit probably lies in the chaotic and random use of customer database marketing practices. For example, a marketing manager may be preparing to send out a direct mail solicitation to target home buyers by mining their database for certain demographics. Although the criteria used for selecting the targets might have been approved by the legal department, there is often no control to ensure that the final query that was used actually conforms to the preapproved criteria. When the campaigns are audited, a racial bias may be interpreted even though it was never intended.

Misrepresentation

With the rapid product rollouts that take place in contemporary business practice, little time is available to marketers to fully review and verify that the information communicated to customers via product packaging, sales materials, and Web sites is consistent and accurate. Dangerous errors may occur. For example, a pharmaceutical marketer may unintentionally give improper dosage information, omit allergy-causing ingredients, or incorrectly label proper product handling instructions. Clearly, these errors could lead to catastrophic results. Less egregious, but still illegal, is the practice of slamming, wherein a long-distance firm changes provider service without the express permission of the customer. The FCC, which began regulating this activity in November of 2000, provides for payments to authorized providers and customers of up to 150 percent of the slammer's phone charges. Even legal, but ambiguous, communication can lead to trouble for direct marketers. In one case, a representative of a major long-distance company induced a homeowner to switch to that company after making claims about the service that the homeowner later learned were false. The situation was not resolved until after the state attorney general's office became involved in the case.

Marketing Expenses

Sarbanes-Oxley requires communication about the effectiveness of internal controls related to financial reporting. Computing systems must protect the integrity of corporate, financial, and customer data. Marketing expenditures represent a significant percentage of overall company costs. Marketing managers are famous for ad hoc, unplanned operating expenses because of market changes and competition. Unfortunately, these unexpected expenses are difficult to report accurately in the financial reports. Corporate profit and loss statements could have margins of error up to 10 percent directly attributed to marketing staff reporting discrepancies. Because of

Sarbanes-Oxley, it is imperative for marketing departments to become financially accountable.[12]

After the corporate scandals of Enron, WorldCom, and Tyco, it should be clear to the managers of both large and small businesses that there are real risks today for not complying with federal, state, and local laws and government regulations. It is imperative to cross the "t's" and dot the "i's." Yes, Sarbanes-Oxley includes you.

Privacy

It is good to note that small businesses do not have to "reinvent the wheel" with regard to privacy and ethics. Perhaps the first source for standards should be a trade association in which the business is involved. As already noted, the DMA sets ethical standards for its members. Any business can use these as a good starting point for its own standards. A privacy policy creation template is available on the DMA Web site. You can also obtain recommendations through the Small Business Administration and local business associations.

When developing a privacy policy, you should include the following:

- A statement of how personal information is used and shared within or outside the company
- Steps to be taken to ensure consumer information is kept secure and private
- Customer choices regarding the use of their information
- A way to contact your company
- An unambiguous message that your firm is willing to discuss privacy issues
- Full disclosure to consumers pertaining to when and why their personal information is collected

It is also important to take a "jurisdictional" approach to compliance activities, including consumer privacy issues. A small business should review the regulatory requirements of each jurisdiction in which it acts. Businesses operating solely in one state—New York, for example—should review federal, New York State, and local regulations. A regional business must review privacy standards in each state, especially if its activities are in states with active legislatures, such as California or Florida.

The *Florez* case provides an illustration. In this case, a court held that a business could not ask for a customer's telephone number before she paid with a credit card. Nothing in the law bars a consumer voluntarily providing a telephone number, but California's law does ban requiring personal information as a condition of a credit transaction. The court ruled that because the telephone number was obtained before the credit card was given, it was implied that the number was required (although it was not actually a required piece of information). The retailer has appealed.[13]

To fully understand the implications for your business, three questions should be asked:

- What types of data do I gather from consumers?
- How do I use or intend to use the data I gather from consumers?
- How long do I retain data I have gathered?

Based on the answers to these questions, you can identify both what data you have gathered in the past, how it was treated, and what changes you might need to make in the future.

Another critical point to keep in mind is that your privacy policy should be designed to protect you from the most litigious individual. In court cases, this is often referred to as the "least sophisticated consumer." When you review statements you make to the public regarding your privacy policy, you should ensure that they are written in a nondeceptive manner such that your least sophisticated consumer can understand their terms clearly.

SUMMARY

In summary, an ethically sound business can be ensured by the following:

- Leading with moral courage
- Adopting standards
- Hiring and promoting the right people
- Creating an ethical culture

Finally, beware of government regulations—they are coming at marketers fast and furious. Laws governing racial bias, misrepresentation, financial reporting and privacy are regulatory landmines that can literally "wipe out" firms that have not protected themselves with high standards of compliance and ethical decision making. By taking the high road, your company not only will avoid needless legal entanglements, but also will enjoy an enhanced reputation, and you will be more likely to sleep with a clear conscience.

NOTES

CHAPTER 1

1. Seth Godin, *Permission Marketing* (New York: Simon & Schuster, 1999).

2. Michelle Toivonen, business development, The Friendly Geeks at Genie Repros, Inc., personal communication.

3. Robert A. MacKay, vice president of Internet sales and marketing, Step2 Corp., personal communication.

4. www.lehmans.com (accessed July 30, 2006).

5. Tim Searcy, CEO, American Teleservices Association, personal communication.

CHAPTER 2

1. "Customer Knowledge Takes Priority in Study," *Marketing News*, December 15, 2005, p. 4.

2. www.harryanddavid.com (accessed July 30, 2006).

3. "Brill's Blog Builds Community and Gets It Right," *Marketing News*, December 15, 2005, p. 23.

4. Cheryl Agronovich, CEO, Wellcorp, personal interview, July 21, 2006.

5. James Barnett, former vice president of North American sales, Goodyear Tire and Rubber Co., personal interview, May 18, 2006.

6. Robert Pacanovsky, founder, Bravo Event Group, personal interview.

CHAPTER 3

1. Jim Collins, *Good to Great* (New York: HarperBusiness, 2001), p. 90.

2. Ibid., p. 91.

3. Ira Davidson, director, Small Business Development Center, Pace University, personal communication.

4. Andre Anthony, owner, Cougar Electronics, personal communication.

5. www.consumerreports.org/cro/cars/index.htm (accessed July 30, 2006).

CHAPTER 4

1. Rupert Murdoch, speech to the American Society of Newspaper Editors, April 13, 2005, available at www.newscorp.com/news/news_247.html (accessed July 30, 2006).

2. Sun Tzu, *The Art of War*, ed. and trans. James Clavell (London: Hodder & Stoughton, 1981), pp. 36–37.

CHAPTER 5

1. Gordon S. Linoff, and Michael J. A. Berry, *Mining the Web: Transforming Customer Data into Customer Value* (New York: John Wiley & Sons, 2001).

2. "Design Forum Uses SPSS Predictive Analytics to Help Dunkin' Donuts Redesign Menu Panel to Suit Its Customers' Tastes," presented at SPSS Directions Users' Conference, Chicago, IL, October 26, 2004.

3. Thomas Pyzdek, *The Six Sigma Handbook: A Complete Guide for Green Belts, Black Belts, and Managers at All Levels*, rev. and expanded ed. (New York: McGraw-Hill, 2003), p. 240.

4. Ashley M. Heher, "Casket Makers Rethink Business Strategy." Associated Press, March 3, 2006.

5. Amy Syracuse, "Co-op Databases Offer Savings, Services for Those Willing to Share," *BtoB Online*, February 13, 2006, available at www.btobonline.com/article.cms?articleId=27054 (accessed July 30, 2006).

CHAPTER 6

1. "The Vanishing Mass Market," *Business Week*, July 12, 2004, available at http://www.nimblefish.com/html/solutions.html (accessed July 30, 2006).

2. Andrew Nibley, "International Media and Marketing in the Digital Age," AMA Meeting, presented at a meeting of the Akron/Canton chapter of the American Marketing Association, Cuyahoga Falls, OH, April 18, 2006.

3. Sarah Johnson, "Trend's So Commercial," *In Marketing*, April 2006, p. 7.

4. www.marriott.com (accessed July 30, 2006).

5. John McCann, "The Co-Marketing Paradox," available at www.duke.edu/~mccann/cpg/scanmktg.htm (accessed July 30, 2006).

6. Ibid.

7. Ibid.

8. Tamara Brezen Block and William A. Robinson, eds., *The Dartnell Sales Promotion Handbook*, 8th ed. (Chicago: Dartnell Corp., 1994).

9. Steve Albrecht, president, Albrecht, Inc., personal interview, August 1, 2006.

10. "E-Mail Lists Getting Cheaper and More Home Grown," *In Marketing*, February 2006, p. 9.

11. Harvey Nelson, cofounder, Main Street Gourmet, personal interview, August 4, 2006.

12. "Radar Screen," *In Marketing*, February 2006, p. 8.

13. "RSS: Find Data and Feed It," *In Marketing*, February 2006, p. 8.

14. Available at http://blog.digitalimpact.com/marriott/ebreaksrss.html (accessed on April 1, 2006).

15. "800-Pound Guerrilla," *Marketing News*, April 15, 2006, p. 15.

16. Christine Blank, "PGA Swings for Higher Show Attendance," *Direct Marketing News*, January 23, 2006, p. 10.

17. Andrew Nibley, "International Media and Marketing in the Digital Age," AMA Meeting, presented at a meeting of the Akron/Canton chapter of the American Marketing Association, Cuyahoga Falls, OH, April 18, 2006.

18. Anastasia Goodstein, "Ypulse Essentials," July 21, 2006, http://ypulse.com/archives/2006/07/21/index.php (accessed July 30, 2006).

19. Elinor Mills, "Advertisers Look to Grassroots Marketing," *ZDNet News*, April 4, 2006, available at http://news.zdnet.com/2100-9595_22-6057300.html (accessed July 30, 2006).

20. www.lastminutedeals.com (accessed July 30, 2006).

21. Andrew Nibley, "International Media and Marketing in the Digital Age," AMA Meeting, presented at a meeting of the Akron/Canton chapter of the American Marketing Association, Cuyahoga Falls, OH, April 18, 2006.

22. *Advertising Age*, July 2, 2001, vol. 72, issue 27, page 1.

23. James Hibbard, "Team Branding," *Television Week*, October 11, 2004, p. 2.

24. Carla D'Nan Bass, "Strategy Puts Consumers in Groups," *Akron Beacon Journal*, October 9, 2000.

CHAPTER 7

1. Barry Berman and Joel R. Evans, *Retail Management: A Strategic Approach*, 9th ed. (Upper Saddle River, NJ: Prentice Hall, 2004), pp. 78–79.

2. Kerry Capell, "Ikea: How the Swedish Retailer Became a Global Cult Brand," *Business Week*, November 14, 2005, p. 98.

CHAPTER 9

1. Joel Sobelson, former chief creative director, Wunderman New York, personal communication.

CHAPTER 11

1. "Nordstrom Tops the Customer Service List," *Chain Store Age*, November 15, 2005, available at www.retailnet.com/story.cfm?ID=25237 (accessed July 30, 2006).

CHAPTER 12

1. Roger J. Best, *Market-based Management: Strategies for Growing Customer Value and Profitability* (Upper Saddle River, NJ: Prentice Hall, 1997).
2. Ruth P. Stevens, *Trade Show and Event Marketing: Plan, Promote, and Profit* (Mason, OH: Thomson, 2004).

CHAPTER 13

1. Geoffrey Colvin, "America Isn't Ready (Here's What to Do About It)," *Fortune*, July 25, 2005, available at http://money.cnn.com/magazines/fortune/fortune_archive/2005/07/25/8266603/index.htm (accessed July 30, 2006).
2. "Brill's Blog Builds Community and Gets It Right," *Marketing News*, December 15, 2005, p. 23.
3. M. David Dealy and Andrew R. Thomas, *Change or Die: How to Transform Your Organization from the Inside Out* (Westport, CT: Praeger, 2005).
4. Arundhati Parmar, "DM Top Method to Reach Pharma Buyers," *Marketing News*, October 27, 2003, pp. 4–5.
5. Michael Fielding, "Get Circulation Going," *Marketing News*, September 1, 2005, pp. 9–10.
6. Allison Enright, "E-bill Pay Creates DM Hurdles," *Marketing News*, September 1, 2005, p. 11.
7. Linda M. Foley, Douglas W. Vorhies, and Victoria D. Bush, "Organizational Learning and Dynamic Marketing Capabilities: Implications for Organizational Performance," *Proceedings of the AMA Winter 2005 Educators Conference*, ed. Kathleen Seiders and Glenn B. Voss (Chicago: American Marketing Association), pp. 138–39.
8. Jack Welch, "It's All in the Sauce" (book excerpt), *Fortune*, April 18, 2005, pp. 138–44.
9. Sun Tzu, *The Art of War*, ed. and trans. James Clavell (London: Hodder & Stoughton, 1981), pp. 97–98.

CHAPTER 14

1. Beth Negus Viveiros, "Call at Your Own Risk," Direct Magazine, July 1, 2005, available at http://directmag.com/mag/marketing_call_own_risk/index.html (accessed July 30, 2006).

2. John and Suzanne Morse, "Teaching Temperance to the 'Cookie Monster': Ethical Challenges to Data Mining and Direct Marketing," *Business and Society Review*, vol. 107, no. 1 (2002), pp. 76–97.

3. Ibid.

4. Pat Kachura, senior vice president for ethics and consumer affairs, Direct Marketing Association, personal communication.

5. Ibid.

6. www.the-dma.org/guidelines (Accessed July 30, 2006).

7. Ibid.

8. Don Oldenburg, "A Bagging of Tricks," *Washington Post*, January 15, 2006, p. F5.

9. Woodstock Theological Center, *Creating and Maintaining an Ethical Corporate Climate: Seminar in Business Ethics* (Washington, DC: Georgetown University Press, 1990).

10. United States v. FMFG, Inc., civil action no. 3:05-CV-00711, FTC file no. 0423155, January 6, 2006.

11. Don Oldenburg, "A Bagging of Tricks," *Washington Post*, January 15, 2006, F05.

12. Sarbanes-Oxley Act of 2002, Pub. L. No. 107-204, 116 Stat. 745.

13. Florez v. Linens 'N Things, Inc., 108 Cal. App. 4th 447, April 30, 2003.

INDEX

ABOUT THE EDITORS AND CONTRIBUTORS

STEVEN BRUBAKER is senior vice president of corporate affairs for InfoCision Management Corp., where he serves as the company's spokesperson for media-related news and public relations events, oversees InfoCision's continued expansion and the deployment of all new call centers, and directs the company's department of regulatory compliance. A member of several professional organizations, including the American Teleservices Association and Direct Marketing Association, he is a frequent guest speaker for industry events. He has also contributed to numerous industry trade journals and publications, including *Call Center Magazine, Customer Interaction Solutions, DM News, DMA Insider, DMA Teleservices Council Newsletter, Fundraising Management*, and *Journal of the American Teleservices Association*.

MARK COLLINS is the creative director at Suarez Corp. Industries. At SCI he oversees a creative staff responsible for more than $100 million in annual sales. Since 1997, Mark has instructed a course in direct marketing and copywriting at the University of Akron.

ANN DAHER FLEMING is an accomplished marketing professional who has developed and executed global product development and market strategies for multibillion dollar corporations in health care, consumer, and industrial businesses. Her experience includes the relaunch of mature products into new markets, product enhancements, product line extensions, and product line rationalizations at Fortune 55 companies such as Avery Dennison. In her practice, Ann Fleming & Associates, Ltd., she directs product and market development for companies and startup businesses.

LINDA M. FOLEY is assistant professor of Marketing at the University of Akron. She is the editor of *Company and Customer Relations*, part of the four-volume set *Marketing in the Twenty-first Century* (Praeger, 2007). Her primary research area is strategy, with a specific focus on learning, innovation, and marketing capabilities. Dr. Foley has conducted academic research and business consulting in selling and sales management, sports marketing, and political marketing, and has done consulting work for several businesses, including Fortune 500 companies and nonprofit companies. Additionally, Dr. Foley served as assistant marketing director for Warner Bros. Records in Nashville, and in a variety of managerial capacities in the finance and restaurant industries.

WILLIAM J. HAUSER is program coordinator for the Taylor Institute and Assistant Professor of Marketing at the University of Akron, where he teaches courses in creative marketing, marketing analytics, and marketing research. He has also taught at West Virginia University and Washington University in St. Louis and is an adjunct associate professor of sociology at the University of Akron. Over the past 20 years, he has served as the manager of market research and business development for Rubbermaid, Inc., and its Little Tikes subsidiary, and, most recently, as senior vice president and director of research & planning for KeyCorp in Cleveland, Ohio (the 13th largest bank in United States). Bill has also completed numerous consulting projects for small businesses and social agencies.

BRUCE D. KEILLOR is coordinator of the American Marketing Association's Office for Applied Research—Direct Marketing and professor of marketing and international business at the University of Akron. He is also a research fellow at Michigan State University. Dr. Keillor specializes in international marketing strategy and direct/multichannel marketing and has authored more than 60 articles published in journals worldwide. He has also contributed to numerous books and is currently chief editor of the four-volume set *Marketing in the Twenty-first Century* (Praeger, 2007). In addition to his academic credentials, Dr. Keillor has also been an active entrepreneur as co-owner of a direct marketing software company he helped found in 1994. Dr. Keillor also has extensive executive education and consulting experience as a copartner in BBA Associates, a global marketing consulting firm.

DALE M. LEWISON is founding director of the Taylor Institute for Direct Marketing and professor of marketing at the University of Akron. He is the author of *Retailing* (6th ed.), *Essentials for Retailing*, and *Marketing Management* (2nd ed.).

CATHY L. MARTIN is a professional educator who has devoted her career to the training and education of individuals in the areas of mathematics, statistics, quantitative business analysis, marketing, integrated marketing communications, buyer behavior, and introductory business. She has taught at the instructor level for more than 25 years at a number of institutions, including the Department of Marketing at the University of Akron. She currently resides in Perth, Western Australia.

KAREN NELSEN has worked at the University of Akron since 1985, and she joined the Department of Marketing in 1990. She coordinates the department's scholarship program and serves on the College of Business Scholarship Committee. Before coming to the university, she worked for more than seven years at a weekly newspaper in Canal Fulton, Ohio, serving as editor for more than two years. Karen also designed and wrote several newsletters for various organizations. She is an artist who works in pastels.

DEBORAH L. OWENS is associate professor of marketing and international business at the University of Akron. Her primary research interests include promotion strategies, customer satisfaction, political marketing, and cross-cultural influence on buyer behavior. She has published articles in *Advances in Business Marketing and Purchasing; Case Research Journal; Journal of Consumer Satisfaction, Dissatisfaction, and Complaining Behavior;* and other scholarly journals. Dr. Owens regularly consults to companies on improving their market position and serves on the State School Board for the State of Ohio.

DAN ROSE has 20 years of experience in industry-leading sales, marketing, and communications. In the early 1990s, he capitalized on the Internet's growing commercial applications by launching an award-winning technology firm, later recognized as one of the fastest growing companies in the Midwest by the Case Western Weatherhead School of Management. Rose has successfully built and sold three separate companies in the technology and communications sector, and has been recognized as "Entrepreneur of the Year" by *USA Today*/NASDAQ/Ernst & Young and as Small Business Advocate of the Year by the U.S. Small Business Administration. He is currently the chief executive officer of Precision Dialogue, an online direct marketing firm, and co-owner of THMG, a data analytics marketing firm.

ANNEMARIE SCARISBRICK-HAUSER is senior vice president and manager of Enterprise Business Intelligence at KeyCorp in Cleveland, Ohio, where she is responsible for enterprise information management for the nation's 13th largest banking institution. Before joining KeyCorp, she was the associate director of the Survey

Research Center at the University of Akron. She is currently an adjunct professor at the University of Akron, where she teaches courses in research methods, collective behavior, and emergency management. Over the past 20 years, she has completed more than 125 research projects for a diverse group of internal and external clients, presented papers at numerous domestic and international academic and professional conferences, published articles in a variety of journals, and co-authored a book on applied sociology.

ANDREW R. THOMAS is assistant professor of marketing and international business and director of the Center for Organizational Development at the University of Akron. A successful global entrepreneur, he has conducted business in more than 120 countries on all seven continents. A *New York Times* best-selling author, his books include *Global Manifest Destiny* and *Aviation Insecurity*, and, with M. David Dealy, *Defining the Really Great Boss* (Praeger, 2004), *Change or Die* (Praeger, 2005), and *Managing by Accountability* (Praeger, 2006).

TIMOTHY J. WILKINSON is associate professor of marketing and international business at Montana State University—Billings. He studies export promotion, international market research, and the international aspects of direct marketing. His papers include publications in *Long Range Planning, Journal of Business Research, Journal of International Business Studies*, and *Journal of Small Business Research*.

ABOUT THE TAYLOR INSTITUTE

In 2006, only 39 U.S. colleges or universities reported offering a direct marketing program with at least 50 percent of the course content spent on areas of direct marketing. None of these schools reported requiring hands-on experience with direct or interactive marketing companies.

In response to this deficiency, the University of Akron's College of Business Administration launched the Taylor Institute in the fall of 2004. It did so in partnership with Gary L. Taylor, chairman of the board of Akron-based teleservices company InfoCision Management Corp.

Taylor graduated from the University of Akron in 1975 with a bachelor's degree in business. He served as a graduate research assistant in the Department of Marketing while earning his master of business administration from the University of Akron in 1977. He has more than 25 years experience in direct marketing, fundraising, advertising, and telemarketing. In 2003, the University of Akron presented Taylor with the prestigious Frank L. Simonetti Distinguished Business Alumni Award.

Currently, the Taylor Institute is engaged in cutting-edge research, corporate training, and executive education both in the United States and around the world. In January 2007, the journal *Direct Marketing International* will publish its first edition. Programs designed especially for entrepreneurs are being offered in Eastern Europe and the United Kingdom. And, the Taylor Institute is a preferred training partner for COSE (Council of Smaller Enterprises), one of the world's largest business organizations.

The contributions of high-profile direct marketing practitioners who act as faculty, administrators, and advisors give the institute a unique advantage. The institute offers an e-marketing and advertising major and two minor programs in database marketing and direct interactive marketing. While traditional pedagogies such as lectures, discussions, and case analyses are included in the curriculum, the institute balances theory with practicum by emphasizing internships and hands-on learning in state-of-the-art labs.

THE TAYLOR INSTITUTE FOR DIRECT MARKETING AT THE UNIVERSITY OF AKRON E-NEWSLETTER

Written and published by the marketing faculty of the University of Akron, this is a free monthly e-newsletter that provides news, summaries, analyses, commentaries, and insights on direct marketing research and practice.

The e-newsletter provides timely updates to direct marketing issues, interesting links, and general commentary. Join the more than 10,000 readers who receive direct marketing information from the Taylor Institute e-Newsletter.

To subscribe, please visit http://www.uakron.edu/colleges/cba/institutes/taylor/index.php

The Taylor Institute will not use the e-newsletter mailing list for any other purpose than distributing the newsletter. We will not use the mailing list for product marketing, nor will we sell the list to any third parties.